Teaching is Tough!

A Practical Guide to Classroom Success

Edited by:

Philip Bigler, Stephanie Doyle & Karen Drosinos

APPLERIDGE
PUBLISHERS

First Edition, August 2014

Copyright © 2014 by APPLE RIDGE PUBLISHERS

Apple Ridge Publishers
217 Bob White Lane
Quicksburg, Virginia 22847
http://www.appleridgepublishers.com
http://www.teachingistough.com

ISBN: 978-0-578-14124-4

PRINTED IN THE UNITED STATES OF AMERICA

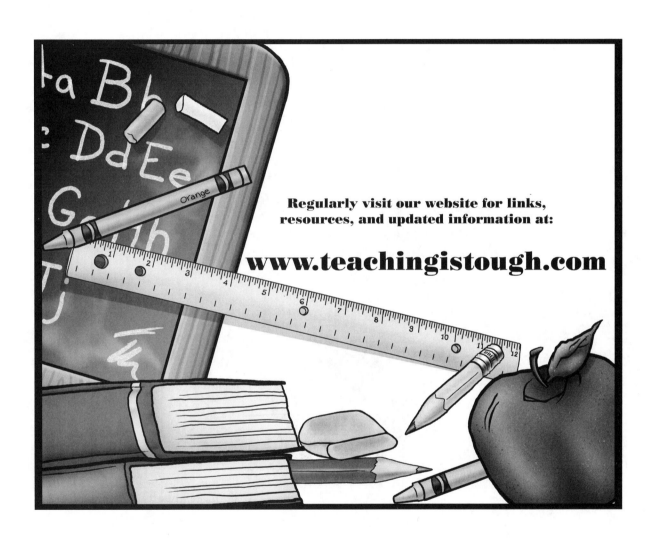

Regularly visit our website for links,
resources, and updated information at:

www.teachingistough.com

A very special *THANK YOU* to the following organizations and universities who have graciously sponsored a variety of VATOY initiatives...

Stock photos were purchased for use from the following sources: Digital Juice, Comstock Images, Corbis Images, Media Focus, Serif, and Dreamstime. The folliwing CD-ROM's of educational photographs were purchased and rights obtained: *Early Ed; Education 1; Higher Ed; Just Teens; School Days; Secondary Ed; and Students and Education.* Other graphic resources, clip art and images were purchased from the Software of the Month Club (SOMC), Digital Juice, and Fotosearch.

Contents

Melissa Porfirio
2014 Virginia Teacher of the Year &
National Teacher of the Year Finalist

Pat yourself on the back and kiss your brain! If you are reading this book, you have decided to become a member of the most essential, dynamic, challenging, and rewarding profession on the planet. Education makes ALL other professions possible. Dietrich Boehnhoffer, an anti-Nazi theologian said, "The ultimate test of a moral society is the kind of world that it leaves to its children." As educators, we are on the front lines of helping our communities and ultimately our world become more just and more equitable. We cultivate critical thinkers who continue to learn, question the status quo, and become tolerant, contributing members of our broader communities and world. Educators have the power to influence countless students to not simply change the world but to transform it. If you are thinking that's one awesome responsibilty, you're right! Never undersestimate the impact you can have on a student's life. Acknowledge that this influence can be positive or negative and take great care to know your students and their families. Get to know the whole child and not just the student in your class. Know what can build them up and what may cause a barrier or devastate them.

The great news is that we are never alone in this profession and we never should be. The Virginia Teacher of the Year (VATOY) Network has written *Teaching is Tough! A Practical Guide for Classroom Success* for this very reason. Gone are the days of teachers heading to their classrooms and closing their doors once students have arrived. In truth, those days were never really meant to be. Just imagine what Lev Vygotsky would say about that isolation! It is thanks to the incredible educators in my graduate program at George Mason University and in my building at Crestwood Elementary School, that I have become the teacher I am. I am also fortunate that my practice can continue to strengthen through collaboration with the VATOY Network and the National Network of State Teachers of the Year. As extraordinary as our role as educa-

Melissa Porfirio, the 2014 Virginia Teacher of the Year (Philip Bigler)

tors is, the reality is that teaching is tough. Having encouraging and knowledgeable allies in your corner can support your efficacy, longevity, and passion for helping students believe in their abilities and all of their possibilities.

Teaching is Tough! is the kind of support that can help you be the exemplary educator you dream to be. While I felt very prepared by my graduate program, had triple licensure under my belt, and felt confident I was going to include families in my classroom and their children's educational journeys, nothing prepared me for that first day when I asked my first grade friend to pick up his pencil, and he looked at me, picked up his purple, plastic ruler instead, broke it in half, and eloquently screamed, "NEVAAAAH!" Throughout the year, he provided me with memorable opportunities to think on my feet, such as the day he decided to chase Canadian geese from our playground out to the main street in front our school. Nope, this one was not mentioned in my preservice training! While you may or may not have a ruler or Canadian Geese incident, you will have your own incredible experiences; and *Teaching is Tough!* is a great guide to have as you begin to navigate through those experiences and help your students reach their maximum potential.

Melissa Porfirio
2014 Virginia Teacher of the Year &
National Teacher of the Year Finalist

The Virginia Teacher of the Year Network

The Virginia Teacher of the Year (VATOY) Network is comprised of past and recent Virginia State and Regional Teachers of the Year, consisting of K-12 educators in public school settings. This organization is designed to recognize excellence in education. Our mission is to increase public awareness of the important and vital role public educators play in our society. Members of our Network extend their impact by providing expertise and assistance to aspiring educators as well as to their colleagues throughout the Commonwealth of Virginia. Our Network complements the Teacher of the Year Recognition program sponsored by the Virginia Department of Education.

The VATOY Network works diligently throughout the year to organize and implement professional development programs as well as recognize those educators who have recently received the honor of "Teacher of the Year." Our Network collaborates with higher education institutions, to include Roanoke College and Regent University, to elevate the profession through a variety of workshops, professional development conferences, and other opportunities for new teacher mentoring. The VATOY Network partners with Roanoke College to provide breakout sessions at its annual Margaret Sue Copenhaver Institute (MSCI) for Teaching and Learning. In addition, VATOY also partners with Regent University to host the Teaching; Leading; Collaborating Symposium each November for non-continuing contract educators within the Commonwealth's Hampton Roads region.

It is with passion and dedication to the profession that the Virginia Teacher of the Year Network was established. We, as members of the Network, desire to promote our most worthy profession through outreach and collaboration with fellow educators. We strive to meet high expectations in this regard, and are proud to continue the mission of this Network in order to have an everlasting influence on the educational experiences of students in the Commonwealth of Virginia.

Stephanie Doyle
VATOY Chair

Karen Drosinos
VATOY Vice Chair

Chapter I

"Ready, Set - Teach!"

How to Have a Successful Teaching Career from Day One

Congratulations! You have fulfilled all of your college course requirements, finished the required school practicums, completed your student teaching, and received your state license. You can be proud of all that you have accomplished thus far. But now the real work begins. How are you going to become an effective and exemplary classroom teacher?

As we all know, teaching is a wonderful, rewarding profession. Each day poses a new challenge as well as a unique opportunity to inspire and influence students. It is, of course, difficult work and teaching can certainly be unpredictable and sometimes stressful. Yet, no matter how challenging your job may be, it is imperative that you maintain a proper perspective and continue to focus on the important task of educating children. Throughout your career, you should continually work to perfect and improve your craft.

DO:

- *Change*: Great teachers are willing to change and adapt their teaching methods in order to improve. You should be open to new ideas and innovative technologies.
- *Be a Role Model:* Teachers are important role models for their students. Your professional and personal behavior should reflect the highest moral and ethical standards. You should strive to be someone who is both respected and admired. Remember that it is entirely possible that your are the sole positive adult influence in a child's life.
- *Take Pride in Your Profession:* Stop saying, "I'm just a teacher." It takes an enormous amount of skill and talent to motivate and inspire young people on a daily basis. Very few people can actually do this. You need to be an advocate for the teaching profession and take pride in your daily work with children.
- *Have Passion:* There are numerous teaching philosophies and various pedagogical methods but the single common characteristic of truly great educators is that they all believe that what they are doing in school is of vital importance. The best teachers bring an infectious enthusiasm and inspirational passion for learning into their classrooms.
- *Work hard:* The great football coach, Vince Lombardi, once noted that it is only in the dictionary where the word "success" comes before "work." This is sage advice since the best teachers are always working hard, preparing for their classes.
- *Do What is Best for Kids:* Helping children learn should be the cornerstone of your teaching philosophy. No one will ever criticize or argue with you if this is your primary objective.
- *Respect Your Colleagues:* You are not alone in your efforts to educate children. Indeed, you are an integral part of a much larger team that includes school administrators, guidance counselors, clerical staff, cafeteria workers, bus drivers and custodians. You should be polite and respectful to all of your colleagues and co-workers, regardless of their position at the school.

(Media Focus)

DON'T:

- **Be a Foxhole Teacher:** Avoid being the type of educator who merely comes to school, closes his classroom door, and refuses to interact with colleagues or participate in school events.
- **Stagnate:** You should always be doing things to better yourself, including independent reading, additional study, and outside learning. This will improve both your content knowledge as well as your pedagogical skills.
- **Expect to be Perfect:** All teachers make mistakes, and even the most experienced educators can have a bad lesson. During your first couple of years, it is particularly important that you set realistic goals and expectations for yourself. Understand that you are in the process of developing your own classroom personality, and it takes time to become a great teacher. Forgive yourself and strive to have more good days than bad. Learn from past mistakes, but don't dwell on them.
- **Be Thin-Skinned:** Accept criticism and evaluations as positive opportunities to help improve your teaching. Don't take such advice as a personal indictment.
- **Sweat the Small Stuff:** Don't stress about things that are beyond your control. Most teachers who burn out are obsessed by the routine frustrations and bureaucratic responsibilities that are common in all professions. These routine hassles have little to do with actual teaching.

Don't Sweat the small stuff!

(Digital Juice)

Philip Bigler

Things to do in:

- *Visit your classroom to take inventory and to decorate it for the students before school starts.*
- *Obtain your class list. Send a personal note or make a phone call to each of your new students.*
- *Keep current with the latest trends in science and technology. Subscribe to a new magazine such as* Discover *or* Technology Review.
- *Prepare your website for the new year and update it with the first month's calendar and assignments.*
- *Watch an inspirational "teacher movie" (e.g.* Mr. Holland's Opus *or* Stand & Deliver*).*

Day One: My First Day as a Second Grade Teacher

As my roommate Amber and I drive to our new school, an ominous dark cloud seems to loom above us. She shoots me a sideways glance that conveys both her worry and concern. The sky darkens further at an alarming rate and suddenly a funnel cloud begins to spin at a tremendous speed. The highway becomes enveloped in a fog of dust and windswept debris. The cars in front of us begin to lift off the ground while nearby trees are uprooted. Amber spins the wheel in an attempt for us to escape, but it is too late…Startled, I wake up in a pool of sweat. Trying to focus my bleary eyes on the blinking alarm clock, I realize that I have experienced my very first back-to-school nightmare. I still have twenty minutes but I am wide awake now so I crawl out of bed to get ready for my first day of school as a new second grade teacher. I am excited but I am also apprehensive. "How will I do?" "Have I prepared enough?" "Will the children like me?"

About an hour later after a quick breakfast, Amber and I are on the road heading down Interstate 66. Amber will be teaching third grade, and we are at the same school in Prince William County, Virginia. We are eager to greet our new classes for the first time and to begin our career as professional educators. It has been both of our dreams to become teachers since childhood. As a little girl, I had my own pretend classroom set up in my playroom, complete with a school desk, chalkboard, whiteboard and a Bill Nye Science Kit for mom-approved science experiments. My younger sister, Kara, was my disciple and she always sat patiently

My very first day as a teacher! (Jami Dodenhoff)

through my lessons (I take a little credit for her success as a student since she is now studying Computer Science at Virginia Tech). I was able to pursue my goal of becoming a teacher by studying at James Madison University. Both Amber and I graduated with Master's degrees as well as our cherished teaching licenses.

During the ride to school, I am overwhelmed with anxiety and fear. I am fully aware of the enormous responsibility I have to educate children, and I want to do my best. I am concerned that my carefully prepared lesson plans will fail to motivate the children, and they will react by taking over my classroom without any concern for their helpless teacher. I also fear the dreaded cafeteria duty and the important dismissal procedures. Most of all, I worry that there has been a mistake—that I am not actually a teacher and that I don't belong here. Amber quiets my fears and reassures me, but we both are feeling a bit uneasy.

We arrive at school very early. Most of the veteran teachers are still at home, but we go over our lessons again and make a final check of our classrooms. Finally, the opening bell of the new school year rings, and I stand outside my door waiting to welcome my kids. Two of my teammates from across the hall cheerfully greet me. They ask me whether I am more nervous or excited. "I'm both," I reply, as groups of eager children filter down the hallway. They are well-

First year teacher, Amber Smith.
(Jami Dodenhoff)

(Comstock Images)

dressed in their new back-to-school clothes and come to class with their coveted princess and superhero backpacks, equipped with bags of supplies. Finally, a little seven year old girl bounces down the hallway and stops right in front of me. "Are you my teacher?" she asks with a toothless grin. "Yes, I am your teacher."

Several days later, I had the opportunity to call a parent of one of my students. I asked her if her daughter liked coming to school. She responded, "Oh, yes! She loves school and every day she comes home and tells me that she wants to be a teacher. She then goes upstairs and pretends to be a teacher for fun. She is so happy." And so am I.

Jami Dodenhoff

My classroom, ready to go on the first day of school. (Jami Dodenhoff)

Classroom Set-Up
It's Worth Thinking About

(Elementary)

As a teacher, you are anxious to transform your classroom into an inviting, efficient, comfy, and warm learning space. Once all of your materials, posters, and books have been arranged, a feeling of panic naturally comes over you as you survey the stacks of cartons and boxes filled with exciting learning materials. You wonder, "Is there enough space?" "How will I set up the classroom so my students will be engaged in their own learning?"

Before you despair, pause and take a moment to think about your student-learners and seriously consider what items they will need and assess the objectives for each area of your classroom.

(Comstock Images)

DO:

- *Investigate your class list*: Check with past teachers, read cumulative folders, and make sure you are setting up to meet the needs of your students. Does one student need special seating, more space, and/or a buddy? Can you use tables, or do you need individual desks?
- *Look at your room from your students' perspective*: This means you will need to get on your hands and knees to survey the room from their level. Make sure you set up your room with their needs in mind. Paper, manipulatives, free choice books, crayons, pencils, and scissors should be strategically placed where they can be reached by students independently.
- *Think thematically*: This will entice your students to explore and will set a tone of cohesiveness and order. Think about your room as a valuable teaching tool. Adding environmental print and a word wall as references will enhance student learning. An added benefit of this is that your students will learn a whole new vocabulary based upon your theme when it is incorporated into everything you do.
- *Organize spaces for students*: Include a place for students to check in, make lunch choices, and turn in bus notes or other important papers. Also, have a system for collecting or turning in work categorized as *in-progress*, *completed*, or *needs to be improved*. This provides your students with an opportunity to become independent and develop a sense of responsibility. Students will also need quiet places and areas that encourage exploration.

DON'T:

- *Underestimate the time needed to plan, create and organize your room*: If you are setting up during your back to school week, keep in mind that this week is usually filled with administrative duties including pre-scheduled professional development, reviews of the faculty handbook, and grade level meetings. Check your school calendar in advance, and plan accordingly.
- *Position computers near windows*: The glare from the sun may make it difficult for the students to read the computer screens.
- *Forget about setting up a whole group teaching area*: This area requires lots of space for students to sit and listen or to move around during instruction. If you have an interactive whiteboard, it may be best to put this area close by, so they can see the board.
- *Fear, worry or rush*: Make your classroom a part of you. If you are happy with your physical space, your students will sense this and they will enjoy learning in their new cozy, safe, warm learning space.

Suzi Sherman

Back-to-School Night

(Elementary)

Back-to-school Night is an extremely important opportunity for you to meet your new parents and students. It is your chance to make that very essential "first impression" as a classroom leader and as a professional educator. It is important that you are well-prepared and ready to share pertinent information with your parents. This should include critical information on school procedures, curriculum, expectations, and appropriate contact information.

Most schools schedule their Back-to-School Nights (sometimes referred to as an Open House in the elementary grades) prior to the start of school or during the first weeks of the school year. You should view this time as an opportunity to create strong and supportive parent partnerships. One of your goals should be to "set the stage" for establishing a positive learning environment. Likewise, you should make your students and parents comfortable and enthusiastic for their exciting learning adventure.

(Serif Premium Images)

10

DO:

- *Greet your students, then your parents*: Your students are your primary focus, and it is important to greet them at the classroom door and personally invite them in to their new learning environment. Their parents will appreciate seeing that your attention is focused primarily on their children.
- *Have important information ready to go*: Essential school papers (bus information, emergency contact information, etc.) should be prepared and filled out during Back-to-School Night. Have all the necessary documents neatly organized in a folder and be sure to designate which materials need to be completed immediately and which items can be returned at a later date.
- *Create a PowerPoint*: As you begin your classroom orientation, it is beneficial for parents to view a well-prepared and thoughtful PowerPoint presentation. A copy of your presentation for the parents should be available online for future reference.
- *Create an organized and inviting classroom environment*: Your classroom is a critical teaching tool, and your students should be excited about learning in their new "home." Have student names printed on all items. Invite students to explore and find their learning spaces identified by personalized name tags. Allow time at the end of your presentation for a classroom "walk about" where students and parents can explore all of the materials, resources, and items in their new learning environment.
- *Provide a unique "take away" for your students*: Always make a personal gesture by providing something special for your students to take with them as a token of their new year. It may be a personal note, a postcard, or even a popcorn bag with a note saying: "Thanks for Popping In!" Be creative and get your students excited about the upcoming school year.

DON'T:

- *Dress unprofessionally*: Back-to-School night is the only opportunity that you will ever have to make a positive first impression. Be sure to dress professionally since this will set the tone for the year. Remember, you are a role model to your students.
- *Complain about school policy or curriculum*: Even though there are always issues and problems that challenge teachers in the ever changing field of education, you should never vent or complain to parents. You want to present all information in a positive manner as a representative of the school.
- *End early/late*: The night goes by very quickly but it is imperative that you use your time wisely. Parents will appreciate you being organized and succinct while respecting the assigned schedule. Fill the designated period but avoid going over your time limit.

Karen Drosinos

Back-to-School Night

(Secondary)

M̲ost public school systems schedule their Back-to-School Night activites in early September. This is an important opportunity for parents to visit the school, and to meet their children's teachers for the first time. During the evening, the parents will want to learn about their child's schedule, course content, and their individual teacher's expectations.

Although your first Back-to-School Night can be intimidating, you should view the night as a unique opportunity to welcome the parents to your classroom. It is also a critical time to elicit their support in your efforts to educate their child. With adequate thought and preparation, it will help set a positive tone for your classes.

DO:

> *"Back-to-School Night" is a critical time to elicit parental support in your efforts to educate their children.*

- *Dress professionally*: As a classroom teacher, you are a well-educated, skilled professional. It is important that this is conveyed to parents through your dress and personal appearance. All teachers should dress conservatively and wear business attire for back-to-school night. A good rule is to dress as if you were interviewing for a new job. It is vital that you make a strong, positive first impression when meeting parents.
- *Greet the parents and students as they arrive*: Teachers should stand at the door and welcome each and every parent and visitor as they enter the room. It is an important opportunity to briefly introduce yourself, shake their hand, and provide them with your course handout. It is, however, not a time to engage in long conversations, so after you have met each parent, ask them to take a seat in the classroom. The parents will then have an opportunity to scan your handout prior to the beginning of the evening's activities.
- *Prepare a class handout*: All parents should receive a handout regarding your class. This will give them an opportunity to review the material more thoroughly when they return home. It is also nice to include a "Dear Parent/Guardian" letter. This letter should be used to formally introduce yourself by providing background information (including your university degrees and education). It should also convey your excitement for your course material and thank the

Be organized and well-prepared on Back-to-School night. Always present a professional and competent appearance. (Media Focus LLD)

parents for allowing you the opportunity to teach their child. It is important that you sign each letter to make it more personal. In addition, you should provide another handout which includes a brief course syllabus summarizing your content, goals, expectations, and rules. It is imperative that, as with all parental communications, that your handouts are grammatically correct and do not contain any typographical errors or misspellings.

• *Have an inviting classroom*: Your physical classroom is an important learning tool and should be clean and aesthetically pleasing. Be sure to have neat, visual, and interesting bulletin boards decorated with appropriate educational materials, posters, pictures, and examples of student work.

• *Fill the entire period*: Most class periods for Back-to-School Night are short, but it is still important to have enough material to fill the entire period.

• *Prepare a PowerPoint*: Parents are interested in seeing what occurs in your classroom. An effective way to showcase your instruction is by using PowerPoint to create a short visual slide show of your classroom activities.

• *Provide contact information*: You should provide parents with information about how to contact you, including your school's email address. Assure parents that you will respond to their digital requests as soon as possible. Remember, though, that all teacher-generated emails represent official school communication. Also, provide parents with your class website information and remind them that they can see the class calendar there as well as find out important information about regular class assignments, reading lists, and activities.

• *Have the parents complete a family information card*: Ask parents to fill out an information sheet and to return it to you at the end of the class period. This card should contain parental contact information and email addresses. Also, ask them to provide information that they would like you to know about their child. This could be something about their child's personal interests, athletic activities, or special needs. This will give you valuable insight and help you effectively teach their child.

• *Say "Thank You"*: Remember that parents are busy people and that it took a good deal of effort for them to come to Back-to-School Night. Thank them for attending and for taking such an important interest in their child's education.

Check out comedian Don McMillian's video on YouTube entitled "Life after Death by PowerPoint." He shows with humor the common mistakes that people make when making presentations. See his website at http://www.donmcmillian.com.

DON'T:

- *Talk about individual students*. Back-to-School Night is devoted to talking about your program, objectives, and goals and is not designed for parent conferences. If a parent asks about an individual child, politely inform them that you would be happy to schedule a parent conference with them at a later date.
- *Overemphasize policies and procedures*. Too many teachers waste time reading over their rules for the classroom. The overall tone for Back-to-School night should be positive and enthusiastic rather the legalistic. Parents can read your class rules in your prepared handout.
- *Complain*. Never share your problems or issues with parents. This night should never be used as a public forum to air any complaints or your dissatisfaction with school.
- *Share social media information*. Never "friend" parents on social media outlets. These are not to be used for professional contacts, and it is important that you maintain a proper relationship with parents and students.

Philip Bigler

It is important to celebrate all of your students' birthdays over the course of the school year. **The Birthday Chronicle** is an inexpensive piece of software that allows you to print customized "This Day in History" certificates. Be sure to acknowledge all of the summer birthdays during the last week of school so that everyone gets appropriately recognized.

NEVER share PERSONAL INFORMATION OR social Media with PARENTS OR students

(Comstock Images)

Sample of a Parent/Student Information form for Back-to-School Night

Parent/Student Information Form

Please fill out the form below. All information will be considered *confidential*.

Student's Name: _____

Date of Birth (including year) _____

Parent(s) Name: _____

Email Address: _____

Best Telephone #: _____

Are you willing to chaperone class field trips or activities?   Yes No   Maybe

Please tell me one important thing I should know about your child.

Are there any health concerns that I should be aware of?   Yes (explain)   No

What is your child's favorite book? movie? television show? sporting activity?

Do you have any recommendations or contacts for guest speakers?

Any additional comments?

Meet Your School's Counselor

School counselors are an integral part of the school system. They provide services that support students' academic, personal, social, and future career development. By offering individual and group counseling, as well as classroom lessons for your students, counselors are ultimately helping to make students more effective learners. Many students come to your classroom from difficult backgrounds characterized by chaotic and unstable home environments, while others are battling mental health issues or learning disabilities that make it difficult for them to learn. Students thrive from the routine and consistency of your welcoming classroom environment, but there are times when external factors make learning difficult for them. In these situations, school counselors become your biggest ally and can offer support by addressing the student's needs and supporting you both in the process.

DO:

- ***Refer students for services***: If you have academic, behavioral, emotional, or social concerns about a student, refer them to your school counselor for help. The counselor will gather information from you, the student, and the parent in order to work together to support the student.
- ***Take advantage of group counseling opportunities***: School counselors frequently offer weekly small groups throughout the year on a variety of topics that help students feel supported while achieving growth and development in a particular area. These groups might focus on test anxiety, study skills, grief and loss, divorce, friendship, self-esteem, or getting along with others. Take advantage of group opportunities for your students. Be flexible when arranging a time that counselors can meet with students.

(Comstock Images)

- *Consult when you are stuck*: Students may struggle with a number of different problems that disrupt the learning process. If you have tried several interventions without progress, consider consulting your school counselor. Together, you can explore other possible solutions to whatever issues you are facing.
- *Ask for help when dealing with difficult parents*: School counselors are trained to communicate with others about sensitive topics. If you feel uncomfortable meeting with a parent alone, ask your school counselor if she can join you and offer their expertise at the meeting.
- *Collaborate on school-wide programs*: Counselors often coordinate valuable, exciting school-wide initiatives that promote positive behavior and important character traits. Working with your counselor on these projects will give you an opportunity to help improve your school culture, which contributes to a more productive learning community.
- *Take care of yourself and ask for help if needed*: The first few years of teaching can be overwhelming, stressful, and draining. Remember to take care of yourself and develop a healthy self-care routine including regular exercise and relaxation. Visit your school counselor if you find yourself feeling burnt out and exhausted.

DON'T:

- *Wait too long to refer students for services*: Counseling is designed to be preventative in nature, so it is important to let counselors know about your concerns as soon as possible. Documenting and sharing your concerns about a student early on will make it more likely for interventions to make a positive change in the child's life.
- *Send students to the counselor for discipline*: In order for students to have an accepting, trusting relationship with their school counselor, it is imperative that they never be sent to the counselor's office for discipline.
- *Expect a magic fix*: It can take time to determine the root of any behavioral or emotional concerns and often several interventions need to be tried before progress is made. In addition, counseling can be a lengthy process and school counselors sometimes have to refer students to a mental health professional outside of school for more intensive long-term intervention. Be patient and trust the process.
- *Assume that counselors can tell you everything students disclose*: School counselors are required to protect the confidentiality of students that they meet with, unless they are worried about a student's safety. There will be times when counselors cannot tell you every detail of what a student is experiencing. However, they will give you as much information as they are able to so that you can be informed as one of the most important people in the child's life.

Katie Overstreet Ruscito

When To Call Counselor 911!

Student safety is a number one priority and there will be times when you need to refer students to the school counselor immediately if you are concerned about their safety. All schools have reporting procedures for these types of situations, so make sure you clarify the procedure in your building before school starts. If you ever have any reason to suspect one of the following crisis situations, call your school counselor or an administrator immediately:

The student discloses thoughts about wanting to hurt himself.

The student makes a threat to hurt others.

You suspect possible child abuse at home.

(Serif Premium Images)

Twenty Important Roles and Responsibilities of School Counselors

1. Provide *individual and crisis counseling* on a regular basis to help meet the needs of all students.

2. Organize small *group counseling* opportunities for students.

3. *Communicate with parents* regularly about student concerns and progress.

4. *Consult* with teachers and staff members to help students succeed.

5. Plan and facilitate regular *classroom guidance* lessons on developmentally appropriate topics.

6. Guide students through the *career exploration* process. Create and maintain Academic Career Plans with all students in grades 7-12.

7. Lead students and parents through the *college application process.*

8. Meet with students individually or in small groups to provide *academic advising* and assist with course scheduling.

9. Work in partnership with the school registrar to *enroll new students*, review student files, and maintain student records.

10. *Coordinate school-wide programs* such as Bullying Prevention, Character Education, Student Recognition, and Community Service Learning.

11. Assist with and help coordinate *school-wide testing*.

12. Utilize *community outreach* to educate parents and the local community on important topics such as Internet safety, cyber bullying, or parenting skills.

13. *Help needy families* to access basic necessities in the community such as food, clothing, and school supplies.

14. *Refer students for services* outside of school such as counseling, mentoring, Big Brothers/Big Sisters or other helpful interventions.

15. *Collaborate with outside agencies* to support students such as social services, psychologists, psychiatrists, and counselors.

16. Regularly participate in *student support teams* such as child study, 504, eligibility, or IEP meetings.

17. Serve on or lead the school's *Crisis Team,* which responds to school tragedies such as the death of a student or staff member.

18. *Focus on the accountability of the counseling program* by utilizing pre/post tests and surveys to gather data, analyze results, and share progress with key stakeholders.

19. Participate as a member of *staff team meetings* that coordinate the daily operations and goals of the school.

20. Take advantage of *continuing education* opportunities in order to stay current in the field of counseling.

...AND SO MUCH MORE!

Getting to Know the School's "VIPs"

As a member of a school faculty, you will be spending a large amount of time with your new colleagues. They will assist, guide, support, and lead you through your career. There is another group of school professionals that you will also be working with, and it is important to meet and appreciate them as well. These individuals are often labeled as the "support staff" since they are not involved in direct instruction. But they, too, are instrumental in helping children learn by assisting teachers. Respect and cherish them.

This list of support staff is large. It includes the office secretary, the finance officer, custodial workers, school nurse, counselors, cafeteria staff, resource officers, aides, maintenance workers, computer technicians, and bus drivers. These school employees are responsible for the day-to-day operation of the school and they offer important support to teachers, students, and parents. Their duties range from dealing with phone inquiries to providing nutritious meals to fixing uncooperative computers. Each person has an important responsibility in helping to provide for the basic needs of every student and in creating a safe and efficient environment to engage learners.

DO:

- *Introduce yourself*: Get to know all of the school's staff and familiarize yourself with their roles and responsibilities. It is important for teachers to know who to call upon for specific services. Remember that they, too, are very busy so you do not want to waste their time. Be courteous and friendly; learn their names and greet them cheerfully each day. A friendly "hello" coupled with a smile helps show your appreciation.
- *Find out their birthdays*: Send a personalized card to these colleagues and celebrate their work, especially on your district's "staff appreciation day." It is also important to have your students show proper respect for the school staff by thanking them regularly for their hard work. This will have the added advantage of instilling in your students a sense of individual responsibility.

- ***Notify the school staff promptly when problems arise***: It is always important to address problems in a timely manner. Be sure to communicate to the appropriate staff members what your expectations are and what exactly you need done. This allows them to formulate a plan to help you. Remember, you are all a part of the same team so if there is something that you can do to assist them, DO IT!

DON'T:

- ***Take the staff for granted***: Ocassionally, the school's support staff feels under-appreciated. Remember that a school is a complex operation and it takes the efforts of many individuals for it to run efficiently.
- ***Assume***: Just like teachers, the school staff has long "to-do" lists. Be sure to follow your school's protocol for getting things done. This means following the "chain-of-command" and filling out the proper forms. Most schools, for instance, have on-line maintenance procedures and computer repair forms that are required to be completed before someone can be dispatched to your room. There are also explicit procedures that are outlined in the faculty handbook. Be sure to refer to this before seeking help.
- ***Forget to say thank you***: The school staff does a lot for you and your students. Their jobs are vital to the smooth operation of a school. Establishing positive relationships with this invaluable group of school professionals will have lasting benefits and will make the school a better and happier place.

Suzi Sherman

Things to do in:

- *Look at case loads, IEPs, and student information to prepare to meet student needs and accommodate appropriately.*
- *Start smiling and don't stop until June.*
- *Give a baseline assessment for documented yearly student growth. Record this data to be used during the mid-year mark.*
- *Prepare a calendar (either paper or electronic) to record important dates including faculty meetings, after-school activities, and national recognition weeks.*
- *Send home a "Dear Parent or Guardian" letter which introduces yourself and explains your goals for the year. Be sure to sign each letter to personalize it.*
- *Start a school scrapbook for the year.*

Classroom Routines and Procedures

Creating classroom routines and procedures is an essential aspect of your planning prior to the start of school. A classroom with clear and concise expectations will maximize instruction by minimizing unnecessary interruptions. As a teacher, it is important for you to set your expectations about classroom routines and procedures beginning with the first day of school. Moreover, it is imperative that you have a clear plan in place for how you will manage and organize your students.

There are numerous classroom routines and procedures that you need to establish. These typically consist of things such as how to line up and transition within the room as well as throughout the building; organization such as where things belong; how to ask questions appropriately; how to sit safely; and how to work with peers at desks or tables. Setting clear and attainable expectations for classroom routines and procedures are important, but there is also a need to be consistency in your expectations. This will ensure a successful, productive, and happy school year for all.

DO:

- *Have a "home" for everything*: Create a place where all student items belong as well as routines for classroom procedures. These should include things such as what to do when your pencil needs sharpening (always have extra sharpened pencils ready to be used), how to use the restroom (a quiet hand signal will prevent interruptions), or where to put work (a teacher's mailbox). This will help students with organization and consistency throughout the school year.

- *Post routines and procedures visibly throughout the room*: Make sure that all routines and procedures are prominently posted so that students can make easy reference to them especially during times of transition. For younger students, a poem or chant is a great way to help them remember your classroom routines and procedures.

- *Review, repeat, reflect*: Remember to consistently review your routines and procedures prior to tasks. Then, ask the students to repeat them to you, e.g. Teacher instruction: "Mail me your finished work." Student response: "We will mail you our finished work." After the task, reflect with your students on how well they performed. This may need to be done only a few times until students become accustomed and comfortable with a particular routine.

- *Praise and Practice*: Offer praise to your students while they are learning your new routines and procedures. It is also a great idea to practice some transitional procedures (pushing chairs in, lining up, and walking in the hallway). This has the added benefit of providing a practical and much needed "brain break" as well.

DON'T:

- *Expect immediate results*: Remember that students can learn quickly with positive reinforcement and consistency. It may take up to two weeks to teach effectively a behavior, new routines and procedures. Even Rome wasn't built in a day.

- *Forget to give reminders when needed*: Remind students of your expectations prior and during tasks. Giving hand signals (stop sign, thumbs up) and verbal reminders will help those students who may need some extra support.

- *Single out students*: Your main goal each year is to create a healthy classroom climate that is inviting to all students. Just as students learn at different paces, they will learn their new routines and procedures at different times. You are creating a community of learners so if there are students who consistently forget some routines, you can provide them with a peer to give them a subtle "whisper reminder." That way, you create an environment where students are responsible for themselves as well as one another.

Karen Drosinos

Why I Teach!

Kathy Galford

Many people spend a lifetime searching for the right path to take in life's journey. Pursuing a career that will be meaningful and fulfilling can be quite an arduous task, especially for a young person who is just beginning. Therefore, I feel very blessed that many of the early experiences in my life seemed to steer me toward the most rewarding, promising and significant profession I could ever imagine—teaching.

I get affirmations every day in this career which is why I love it. It happens every time a student lights up because he or she "gets it," when I see joy in learning in my students' eyes, when I try a new strategy and it really works, when a struggling student shows progress, and when I run into former students who have grown into successful adults.

Over the past 24 years, I have been blessed to work with students of all levels and backgrounds. I've taught students with learning differences, students who are considered gifted, affluent students, homeless students, foster children, students with physical, behavioral or academic struggles, students with autism, and students new to America who are just learning to speak English. Each one of them has been a precious gift to me, and it is my duty and honor to get to know my students as individuals and help them to reach their highest potential.

My students keep me motivated. Each year, I get a whole new group of wonderful individuals with different needs, personalities and backgrounds. In 24 years of teaching, I have never had two days that were alike. Each day is new and exciting, especially when I'm trying to improve myself as a teacher by trying new strategies and activities. After more than two decades on the job, I still wake up each morning feeling hopeful and excited about the day ahead.

Today, I feel so blessed to be engrossed in a career that I continue to pursue with the same amount of love, enthusiasm, and dedication I felt when I first began. It is my greatest hope that I have made a difference in the world by influencing some of our future leaders. After many years in this profession, I have watched many of my former students grow into productive adult citizens. Some of them have overcome great obstacles to do so, and some of them have credited me as a source of inspiration. This is the greatest possible reward, and it continues to give my life a sense of purpose.

Chapter II

"Creating a Classroom Community"

Creating a Positive Classroom Environment

The idea of a positive classroom environment conjures up images of teachers assisting students and students making behavior choices to ensure success with learning and personal communications. Creating a positive classroom environment encompasses the whole learning environment and is a necessity in order to provide all students an equitable and fair opportunity to thrive. Effective teachers identify and use strategies, that will positively impact their classroom environment. In essence, they develop a recipe for student success by including a variety of "ingredients" into their daily classroom practices, which result in a positive climate for learning.

DO:

- *Accept student input for creation of class rules*: "Ownership of the goal" is a powerful incentive for cooperation. If a school already has a behavior management plan in place, then you will want to customize your classroom plan so that it complements the school's overall program. However, it is still essential that you specify how your rules will work in your own individualized classroom.

- *Review expectations for classroom rules, procedures, and routines*: Review and reinforce your expectations daily. This will have a positive impact on student behavior. It is important to note that modeling the rules, procedures, and routines is necessary to ensure that all students understand what each looks and sounds like. When reviewing your classroom expectations, you can assess student understanding through observation and praise appropriate behaviors.

(Comstock Images)

- ***Differentiate student responses based upon need***: Not every child will respond to every rule in the same way. Build a solid foundation of understanding of classroom rules by using simple verbal and nonverbal signals. This will help students during the learning process. It is important to accommodate all learners by modeling and guiding students in a step-by-step process directed towards achieving your overall expectations.
- ***Be consistent***: Constant reminders and review will ensure that students fully understand what is expected. It is up to the classroom teacher to continuously monitor and praise student behavior. Incentives can be an effective strategy to use when promoting consistent and positive behaviors in the classroom.

DON'T:

- ***Expect perfection***: Teaching and learning are complex processes. It takes time to develop and implement your classroom plan, so it is important that you be prepared for some bumps in the road and not get discouraged. You have the power to create an effective classroom environment, which will be safe for all students and respectful for all learners.
- ***Underestimate your students' potential***: Although it may initially seem difficult, the rules and procedures that you implement at the beginning of the school year will impact your students throughout the year. Have faith that all of your students can be positive contributors to a positive classroom environment. Creating a positive classroom climate only occurs when you set high expectations for your students and support them in reaching their behavioral goals.
- ***Give up***: Every day is a new day. Always look forward with the intent of making positive progress.

Carolyn Lewis

Things to do in:

- *Re-organize seating charts according to your first month's observations.*
- *Revisit classroom rules. Encourage students to add or edit classroom rules in order to personalize them.*
- *Each day of the month, set a goal to make a positive parent communication so by the end of the month, all of your parents have been contacted with a personal call about their child.*
- *Show your school spirit by attending on-school extracurricular event.*
- *Get a pumpkin spice latte!*

Teaching Values

No teacher has the right or the authority to challenge or disparage a child's religious, political, or family beliefs. Educators should concentrate on helping students think for themselves and think critically about important issues. There are certain societal values that schools can teach and should expect their students to follow. These include such things as honesty, civility, tolerance, and diligence. Schools also can require, at a minimum, that students are on time, dress appropriately, use proper language, and demonstrate respect. Virtually all school districts have developed character education programs but there are many ways that teachers can maintain and encourage proper values as a seamless part of their classroom culture.

DO:

- *Be a Role Model*: Teachers should hold themselves to high standards. Remember you may be the only positive adult influence in a child's life. You need to be someone worthy of admiration and emulation.
- *Use Posters*: Display positive value-related posters around the classroom. Discuss these items with the students and explain what they represent. One excellent free source for materials is "The Foundation for a Better Life" where there are dozens of downloadable PDF poster files which highlight such things as "Good Manners," "Honesty," "Excellence," "Team Work," "Learning," and "Persistence." The site also has outstanding videos and audio files which can be used. Educators can also request a free DVD of their public service television and radio advertisements. The website is at http://www.values.com.
- *Celebrate Heroes*: Too often in our society we glorify people for the wrong reasons. We confuse fame with significance by glorifying actors, musicians, and sports figures. It is important that students learn about true heroes, individuals who have done great things and may have had to overcome considerable obstacles. Such people are an inspiration and should be highlighted as authentic heroes.
- *Have a Class Pledge*: Show your expectations for honesty by having an honor code pledge displayed prominently in your classroom. On all tests, examinations, and assignments, have the students sign the pledge before turning in their papers or projects. A sample pledge would be "On my honor, I have neither given nor received aid on this examination/assignment." Other examples are available online.

- *Allow Personal Expression*: Students should be free to express themselves without fear of retribution or penalty. As Thomas Jefferson stated when establishing the University of Virginia, "This institution will be based on the illimitable freedom of the human mind for here we are not afraid to follow truth wherever it may lead, nor to tolerate any error so long as reason is left free to combat it." This enlightened philosophy should be the standard for all public schools.

DON'T:

- *Impose Your Personal Viewpoint*: Teachers are in a position of authority, and students should admire and respect them. They will inevitably believe that you are infallible and that is an enormous responsibility. No teacher should use his classroom as a personal forum to persuade students to think in a particular way, especially about controversial or political issues. Teachers in such subjects as English and social studies should be honest brokers of information and present balanced perspectives without imposing their own personal viewpoints upon students. Students should feel free to express themselves honestly and forthrightly without fear of adverse consequences.

- *Denigrate or Malign*: It is important for teachers to realize the impact their words can have on a child. A positive comment will be remembered forever by a student, while, conversely, a negative remark can also have lasting impact. Students should never be humiliated or belittled. Their school work should never be held up for public criticism.

Philip Bigler

An Authentic Hero

Bethany Hamilton, a talented and competitive surfer, was attacked by a tiger shark while surfing off of the coast of Kauai in 2003. She lost her left arm at the shoulder; Bethany was just 13 years old. Despite the devastating injury, Bethany refused to be discouraged and worked hard at her rehabilitation. Incredibly, she returned to surfing just four weeks after the attack, adjusting to surfing with one arm. Undeterred, she returned to competition and won her first national title in 2004. A few years later, she turned professional.

Her bestselling autobiography, *Soul Surfer*, was made into a feature length movie starring Anna Sophia Robb and featuring Helen Hunt and Dennis Quaid. Bethany's story is featured on the Foundation for a Better Life website under the topic "Rising Above." In her words, "People can do whatever they want if they just set their hearts to it, and just never give up, and just go out there a do it." She is an inspiration and role model to all young people.

(© Paul Topp | Dreamstime.com)

The Foundation for a Better Life

The Foundation for a Better Life is an excellent resource for educators. The organization offers free posters, DVDs, public service announcements, and other resources promoting positive societal values. Many educators assign students a project where they develop their own unique posters and messages using the site's materials as examples.

(Used with permission from the Foundation for a Better Life)

www.values.com

Doing the Right Thing

On April 26, 2008, two Division II schools, Central Washington and Western Oregon, were playing in an important NCAA softball tournament. In the second inning, the WOU Wolves had two runners on base with platoon outfielder Sara Tucholsky at bat. She had only three hits all season but with a 0-1 count, she hit the next pitch over the centerfield wall for her first career homerun. In her excitement, Sara failed to touch first base but when she pivoted to return to the bag, she tore her ACL. Sara collapsed to the ground in agony. As Sara clutched on to first base, the umpire informed the Oregon coach that no one on the WOU team could help Sara and that unless she were able to round the bases, her hit would be reduced to a two RBI single. Without hesitation, the opposition's first baseman, Central Washington's Mallory Holtman, asked the umpire if she and a fellow teammate could help Sara by carrying her around the diamond to help her touch each bag. It was an incredible act of kindness, selflessness, and sportsmanship.

CWU's shortstop, Liz Wallace, jogged over to help Mallory pick up Sara and together they slowly made their way around the bases, stopping at each to allow her to touch the bag with her uninjured leg. The girls had no idea that someone in the stands was videotaping the entire episode and that their story would soon become national news. Mallory and Liz later said that Sara had hit the homerun and that it was only right that she score. Central Washington eventually lost the game and the conference championship by a score of 4-2. Still, the team's head coach, Gary Frederick, was thrilled because his players were honorable and had done the right thing. He said afterwards, with tears in his eyes, "It's emotional. You're proud to be associated with those kids." For teachers, the story of Mallory, Liz, and Sara is not only inspirational but an important life lesson to teach to all students.

Helped injured opponent win.

SPORTSMANSHIP

Pass It On.

VALUES.COM THE FOUNDATION FOR A BETTER LIFE

(Used with permission from the Foundation for a Better Life)

Building A+ Relationships with Students

Respect is a crucial factor in teacher success. On the first day of school, the vast majority of students are polite, helpful, and well-behaved; they expect that their assigned teachers are capable and skilled professionals. Moreover, the students want you to like them and respect them as individuals. Your challenge is to cultivate and maintain this mutual respect throughout the entire school year. To do so, you must conduct yourself in ways that enhance your rapport with students while building positive relationships with your classes.

James Comer, one of the world's leading child psychiatrists, asserts that "no significant learning occurs without significant relationship." The relationship that you have with your students can be the most important factor in their ultimate academic success. Students will work harder and learn better from educators they like and respect.

DO:

> *"No significant learning occurs without significant relationship."* James Comer

- ***Learn all of your students' names during the first week of school:*** Addressing students by their proper names is imperative. This will ensure that they feel valued as individuals. It requires a great deal of effort to learn everybody's name, but it can be done.
  - o Have students create their own individual nameplates/tent-cards to display on their desks.
  - o Create a lesson plan or activity which requires the students to work alone or in small groups. This will allow you to move around the room and focus on learning their names.
  - o On the first day of class, take digital pictures of all of your students holding name cards. Upload the photographs into a mobile app such as Roster Recall (see http://www.trueidapps.com/rosterrecall/), which allows you to view the images as flash cards and to memorize their names quickly and efficiently.
- ***Greet each of your students at the door every day:*** This will greatly enhance your relationship with your students. Before class begins, you have said "hello," asked about sporting events, and given compliments. You have also had a chance to gauge the type of day that each student is having.

- *Thank the students for their attention and participation at the end of every class:* Your honest appreciation helps build relationships and encourages students to continue to exhibit positive behavior.
- *Attend after school extracurricular activities—sports, drama, music, award ceremonies:* This shows that you care about your students. Always recognize and congratulate students on their efforts and extracurricular successes.

DON'T:

- *Share details about your personal life with your students:* Professional educators are mentors and role models. They must maintain appropriate relationships. This means keeping a proper distance as students should never be treated as your friends. It can be appropriate to share your outside hobbies and interests. Other personal information is off limits and your own family issues should never interfere with your teaching.
- *Share social media information or "friend" students on such forums as Facebook or Twitter:* Never post any inappropriate material, photographs, or content on such sites.
- *Try to fake it:* Students can detect a phony immediately. Your teaching persona should be an honest reflection of your natural personality.
- *Be cynical or use harsh sarcasm:* What you say to your students can have a lasting impact. Remember that children have fragile egos that can be damaged easily by a careless or callous word.

(Media Focus)

Susan Catlett

For an inspiring talk on the importance of teacher-student relationships, watch Rita Pierson's "Every Kid Needs a Champion" at www.ted.com. Pierson, a third-generation teacher and educator for 40 years, shares stories and wisdom that will encourage you to connect with your students and partake in what Pierson calls "the sustaining power of relationships."

Creating Resilience

To be resilient means that you have the ability to learn and recover from difficult or trying circumstances. It is an important life principle that also relates directly to teaching and learning. So, how do you create a positive classroom learning atmosphere that promotes resilience and allows for children to learn from their mistakes?

First, it is imperative for you to replace the notion that "practice makes perfect" with the concept that "practice makes progression." How students progress is what should matter most, and you want your students to continually improve. You will need to provide regular opportunities for students to understand that everyone progresses in different ways and in different increments at their own unique pace. Authentic learning takes time and effort. It is important for you to model resilience in your classroom, by recognizing our mistakes and modeling how you can learn from them as you collectively move forward in the learning process.

> **Take Away Tom says No Negative Words allowed here!**

DO:

- **Encourage students to make decisions**: In a classroom where resilience is practiced, students are encouraged to make decisions about their learning. They understand what is expected of them and what is needed to accomplish a task while recognizing that each is moving through the learning at a different rate and in a different way.

- **Remove negative words from the learning environment**: One of the most important things for you to do is to remove all negative or unhelpful words from the classroom. Early elementary teachers can enlist the help of a puppet friend, "Take Away Tom," to assist in this important task. The class should generate a comprehensive list of words that stifle learning such as "I can't, I won't, I don't know how" and feed these noxious phrases to "Take Away Tom." He will "eat" those words and they are forever removed from the learning vocabulary.

(© Filipwarulik | Dreamstime.com)

34

- *Have an "eraser free" classroom*: Another way to alleviate the pressure of making mistakes is to have an "eraser-free" classroom. Remove all erasers from pencils and replace them with an artificial flower, for example. This will allow mistakes to be an acceptable part in the learning process. When a mistake does occur during paper/pencil tasks, encourage the students to circle their mistake. This will help them overcome the stress of making mistakes and it will also provide you with valuable information about the thought process of your students.

DON'T:

- *Expect perfection*: There is no such thing as perfection, even for teachers. Remember that you are members of the learning environment and will make mistakes yourself. Indeed, sometimes the best teaching moments come from students "catching" a teacher's mistake.
- *Encourage perfection; rather, encourage progression*: It is important to emphasize the *process* of learning in the classroom. Students need to partner in their own learning, and understand that it is not a one-way street. You need to create opportunities for students to think of their learning as a "work-in-progress" and edit, revise, and reflect. Students need to accept that they make mistakes but how they make improvements is what is most important.

Karen Drosinos

Things to do in...

- *Prepare for cold and flu season by stocking up on hand sanitizer, tissues, and other items that will contribute to a "germ-free" environment.*
- *Organize assignments and grade information in preparation for parent conferences.*
- *To commemorate Veteran's Day, make cards for those who have or are currently serving our country.*
- *Start a canned food drive to collect necessary items for upcoming winter holidays.*
- *Explore the true history of Thanksgiving from a variety of perspectives.*

Things to do in...

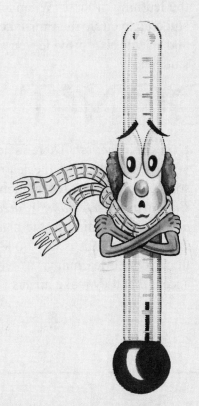

- *Begin looking for a good book to read over the holidays.*
- *Prior to winter break, reorganize your classroom and rid the learning environment of first semester clutter.*
- *Remember to explore all of the winter holidays with students.*
- *Pamper yourself by doing something special. Reenergize your mind and body for the remainder of the school year.*

(Corbis Images)

Chapter III

"The Teacher Toolbox"

Get Out of Your Seats: Engaging Students in an Active Classroom

Gone are the days when teachers expected their students to sit quietly in rows, passive and inactive, never being allowed to get up during a class period. Today, we know that children and adolescents learn best when they work constructively with others, moving around the classroom, while they transition from one engaging activity to another. Having an active and vibrant classroom will be rewarding and exciting for you as the teacher and your students will be enthusiastically involved in content-related conversation, movement, and active learning.

DO:

- *Break up instruction into segments*: Sitting for long periods of time during instruction can be daunting and overwhelm the learners in your classroom. To promote an active learning environment, break up instruction into segments (approximately 10 to 15 minutes in duration) by allowing your students to write on charts, move through learning stations, or sort themselves into groups. This "state change" can support students in stretching their attention span by providing movement and active learning opportunities.

- *Encourage cooperative learning*: Students learn best when communication with their peers is involved. They can freely share ideas, concepts, and learned knowledge with others. Creating opportunities for cooperative learning will increase their learning stamina as well as increase their knowledge base through rephrasing learned information to their peers. (For additional information, consult the works by Johnson and Johnson as well as "Kagan strategies.")

- *Manage your classroom carefully to promote organized activity*: Spend a great deal of time modeling and practicing appropriate ways of listening to others and engaging in conversation. Model and practice organizational procedures with your students often until the procedures become habitual. Display pictures of materials you would like on your students' desks for various activities to avoid having to orally list items.

DON'T:

Nash, Ron. (2009). *The Active Classroom: Practical Strategies for Involving Students in the Learning Process*. Thousand Oaks, CA: Corwin Press.

- *Call on one student at a time*: Allow all class members to discuss and process information at the same time. To check for understanding, ask everyone in the class to turn to a partner and summarize the concept or ask a relevant question while you circulate and monitor the conversations. This is often referred to as "Think-Pair-Share."
- *Expect to transform your classroom immediately*: Do not feel discouraged if this process appears to be difficult. It takes time and preparation to make a positive improvement, so try one active strategy at a time until you are comfortable before incorporating another.

Kathy Galford

Incorporate music into your classroom routines.

Tip!

After you feel comfortable with active classroom strategies, try incorporating music into your daily routine to create mood, manage transitions, and support instruction.

- Quiet classical music is great for settling students at the beginning of class, during creative writing assignments, and focusing during quiet seat work.
- Appropriate upbeat tunes can energize your students as they enter and exit the room and can be utilized (with pauses) to guide students through learning stations or lesson segments.
- Special songs can be used to relate to specific lessons or themes you are teaching. *The Green Book of Songs* (2002) by Subject by Jeff Green catagoriezes thousands of songs by a myriad of topics.

Curriculum Integration

Based on information about brain configuration, current research supports a learning style that integrates instruction of curriculum concepts. Previously, teaching concepts and objectives were treated as separate components and segregated according to subject. This approach allowed for satisfactory skill-based teaching and prepared students to learn the necessary skills that were being taught, but the current mandated assessments are measuring student understanding and require higher-level thinking. Therefore, teachers need to refine their methodology in order to provide more opportunities for students to not only "state the facts" but to internalize concepts, problem-solve, collaborate, and communicate their understanding as well as make connections to the world around them. Curriculum integration is an effective way to teach more than a single objective within a unit of study. Using this approach, teachers will make learning more meaningful and relevant for their students, accomplishing more standards within a course of study.

DO:

- *Plan using backwards design*: Always teach with the final end in mind. Know exactly where you want your students to be and plan backwards to determine how to get them to reach your ultimate goal. A popular approach to this type of curriculum integration can be found in *Understanding by Design*, a book written by Grant Wiggins and Jay McTighe. The authors provide a detailed and thorough description of this approach to curriculum planning.
- *Know the standards*: It is essential that you know and thoroughly understand the required curriculum, standards, and objectives in order to integrate them effectively into a course of study. You, too, must do your homework in order to adequately know what your students are expected to learn. Careful preparation will allow you to create a solid, integrated way to teach the standards.
- *Create thematic units*: Thematic units are designed around a central theme. It is important to know the interests of your students and choose themes that fit their interests, abilities, and curiosities in conjunction with your overall yearly standards and curriculum guides.
- *Incorporate performance tasks*: Performance tasks are an effective way to assess what your students have learned throughout a unit of study by utilizing all of the objectives that were taught through a real-world problem-based activity. This is a fundamental way to culminate a unit of study.

(Comstock Images)

DON'T:

- ***Teach to only one objective***: Curriculum integration is like a stew, with all of its ingredients mixed together, rather than a divided plate with no food touching. Make it messy! Each ingredient corresponds to an objective and true integration occurs when many objectives are mixed together.
- ***Try to "wing it"***: Planning and preparation are key to effective curriculum integration, and they cannot be done quickly or hastily. Lay out all of your objectives by quarter and become organized and familiar with what your students need to learn.
- ***Be afraid to listen to your students***: When creating a curriculum by integrating subjects and objectives, it is important that you listen to your students. Encourage their questions and allow their curiosities to guide your instruction. Sometimes the most effective learning experiences occur when students take the instructional wheel.

Karen Drosinos

Wiggins, Grant and Jay McTighe (2005). *Understanding by Design*. Upper Saddle River, NJ: Pearson Education.

Making It Relevant

The ultimate purpose of education is to prepare students to be lifelong learners and useful, productive citizens. With that in mind, it is every teacher's duty to create an engaging classroom environment which enables our students to see what they are learning in school relates to the world as a whole. Whether in academic subjects or in areas of cooperation and citizenship, it is essential that we strive to tailor instruction so that it becomes meaningful, interesting, and exciting for our students.

DO:

- *Get to know your students*: From the first day of class, find out what is important to your students. Inquire about their individual needs, their personal interests and their hobbies, as well as their family situations. Break the ice by letting your students share some of their personal information through a "getting to know you" questionnaire administered during the first week of school. It will be an invaluable tool in getting to know your students as individuals.

- *Find out how your students learn*: Provide a learning style inventory for each student to take. There are many resources available online as well as numerous examples. This tool will allow students to determine their own learning styles and will help you decide how you can best accommodate the various learning modalities in your classroom. Make sure you share the results of this survey with your students because many of them may not be fully aware of how they learn most effectively.

- *Teach with your students in mind*: Help your students to take ownership of their own learning by providing choices based upon their interests and learning styles. Utilize alternative assessments that allow students to demonstrate their understanding of concepts in ways that engage them personally. You can accomplish this through learning menus, tic-tac-toe grids, choice boards, simulations, and problem-based activities. Also, offer enrichment opportunities such as independent research activities that will allow your students to pursue their own individual interests. Bring difficult concepts to their level of understanding by using metaphors, analogies, mnemonics, songs, raps, and storytelling in your instruction.

- *Put it in real world context*: Teach your students to think like experts in a field of study by having them solve authentic, real-world problems. English students, for instance, should think like writers or editors; social studies students should think like historians, archivists, or museum curators; math students should think like accountants or statisticians; science students should think like biologists, geologists, chemists, or meteorologists. Encourage students to assume these "roles" in class, and you will achieve authentic, exciting learning.

DON'T:

- *Stifle creativity in learning*: Encourage students to be creative by allowing their curiosities to drive your learning activities. It is essential to keep the curriculum relevant for students, and this is done best when students are in the driver's seat.
- *Assume students have a particular skill set*: Learning to think in various ways is not an innate skill; it must be taught and modeled. If you expect your students are to be historians, then you must model, demonstrate, and provide the skills they will need to fully take on that role.
- *Be the leader, rather be the guide*: When beginning instruction on a particular topic, ask your students what parts of that topic they are interested in and would like to investigate further. Although you have a mandated curriculum and know what must be taught, the manner of creating student-learning opportunities is usually at your discretion. The most powerful teaching occurs when your students are involved and can express their interest and curiosities about a given topic.

Kathy Galford

Things to do in:

- *Commemorate Dr. Martin Luther King, Jr. Day by having your students explore prominent civil rights leaders in your town or city.*
- *Create a New Year's resolution as a class community. Display this in your classroom to remind your students of the community goal they established.*
- *Hit the "after-holiday" sales for bargains for your classroom.*
- *Be prepared for snow days. Be ready to adjust your lesson plans accordingly.*
- *Revisit classroom routines, procedures, and expectations.*

Thematic Teaching

Thematic teaching is an exciting teaching method, but it does require an immense amount of planning, organization, and curriculum knowledge. It is always important to look carefully over the schedule for each week and the learning objectives that need to be covered. There are, of course, many options to teach those skills, strategies and objectives.

Thematic teaching is engaging and exciting for both students and teachers. Instead of your time being segmented into rigid time frames by specific subject matter, the day runs seamlessly as it is focused on the same topic. For instance, reading, spelling, writing, math and the arts can be taught using a social studies or science theme. This guarantees that your students will be immersed in the learning process across the curriculum, and your time will be filled with active, motivated and confident students.

DO:

- ***Plan backwards***: Begin your planning by pinpointing what you want your students to know, do, and understand. This backwards planning will help outline the activities that need to be done and the many different modalities of learning that you will need to use.
- ***Utilize your student's strengths***: Knowing your students and their abilities will help you realize what strategies and skills are necessary to develop engaging unit activities.
- ***Relate the unit to your students***: Students will enjoy and better retain their learning if you make it relevant to their everyday lives. This involves building a positive relationship with them. It is important to know their likes, dislikes, family background, and hobbies. Use this information to enhance your daily lessons.
- ***Ask broad questions***: Pose questions for students to ponder during their thematic learning journey. The quest for answers establishes a purpose for the lesson. You will need to provide students with hands-on and minds-on manipulatives for them to investigate. These may include technology, math items, picture cards, art supplies, science tools, maps, and other related fundamental tools for exploration.

- *Point out connections*: Celebrate the connections that your students make during the learning process. Praise them for their higher-level thinking and problem solving strategies. This will increase their confidence and their desire to be involved in other thematic units.

DON'T:

- *Belittle student achievement*: Small, positive observations are the foundation for making strong connections. Acknowledge and celebrate all student ideas and make note of these observations to use in later units in order to foster a deeper understanding.
- *Forget to bring in leveled literature*: You should try to incorporate all genres and types of literature including newspapers, magazines, journals, environmental print, and even cartoons and cereal boxes to supplement your books. Offering a wide variety of related literature will increase students' interest and aid their reading proficiency.
- *Neglect reflection*: Be sure to plan opportunities for your students to reflect upon what they have learned. Did they make any mistakes? Do they have ideas on other ways to explore the topic? Have them create a poster to display their learning.

Suzi Sherman

Things to do in:

- *Celebrate Black History Month by highlighting famous African-Americans who have made an impact in your community and who are relevant to your curriculum.*
- *It's the month of Valentine's Day, a good time to revisit what you "love" about the teaching profession.*
- *Mail a valentine to every student to their home address. Students will love receiving a personalized piece of mail from their teacher.*
- *Commemorate the 100th day of school with your students by celebrating your students' efforts, progress and achievements.*
- *Review September's baseline assessments and goals. Compare data to document student growth.*

Arts Integration

Be Creative

Arts integration should be an integral component in the general curriculum in all American classrooms. Using the term "arts," rather than "art," includes all aspects: fine arts, art aesthetics, art criticism, music, movement, and performance.

Since Arts Education is frequently underfunded in schools, it is important for teachers to expose all students to its various forms of creative expression as a routine component of instruction. Arts integration in the classroom plays an important role in promoting the skills of problem solving, creativity, imagination, and collaboration, and can provide educational experiences for our students to thrive as 21st century learners.

DO:

- ***View and discuss famous artworks and artists***: Use curriculum topics to find well-known artworks that will fit into your learning objectives. Ask the students to view the artwork first by describing what they see—shapes, colors, line variations (art criticism). Then have the students describe how the artwork makes them feel (art aesthetics). Discuss what medium the artist used as well as the title of the work. This provides a great springboard for you to introduce a brief background of the artist and the purpose for the creation of the particular work.

- ***Incorporate music and movement***: Creative movement to music with variations of beats and rhythms can provide enjoyable brain breaks, while giving students the opportunity to hear and respond to different types of music (i.e. jazz, classical, hip hop, polka).

- ***Create a student art gallery***: Use your room to establish a special place to display student art. Frame their special artworks using matting. The student "artists" can write the title of their pieces on the back while their peers can be challenged to submit guesses about the actual topic and title. This reinforces the importance of students' careful attention to the details in artwork.

- ***Retell stories or learning experiences through performance art***: Give students a performance task to create their own play or to retell a story by creating props and organizing a unique performance. This allows students to collaborate and communicate. You will be amazed by their creative products.

DON'T:

- ***Assume craft activities adequately incorporate the arts***: Far too many teachers have the misconception that they are adequately integrating "art" in their classrooms through craft activities. Although craft activities are useful and do reinforce fine motor development and creativity, they are only one narrow component of fine arts. Expand your thinking about arts integration, and you will expand your students' creativity and imagination.
- ***Judge student creations***: Instead elicit positive discussions with your students about how to view art and how to respond to what they see. Encourage students to use descriptive feedback when talking about art ("I like the use of thick lines, but I would like to see more color in the background"). You will need to model this type of feedback in order for your students to become successful in using it themselves.
- ***Be afraid to discuss art, even if you are not an expert***: You do not have to be an art historian or an artist to like or appreciate art. You should enjoy learning and experiencing art along with your students. Be brave and explore the world of the arts and your classroom will come alive in an entirely new way.

Karen Drosinos

"Expand your thinking about arts integration, and you will expand your students' creativity and imagination."

Grading with Rubrics

Alternative assessments are being utilized more frequently as a means of evaluating student progress. By creating effective rubrics, teachers are able to communicate clearly what is expected in an assignment and to grade it more objectively and fairly. This provides students and parents with a better understanding of an assigned grade. Grading with rubrics may initially seem like a confusing and complicated task, but by using the resources available to you and actively involving your students in the process, you will find rubrics to be an effective tool in your classroom.

DO:

- ***Involve your students in the process of creating rubrics***: This will give them a clear understanding of the expectations for an assignment and will allow them to assume ownership of the task. Develop the criteria and discuss the importance of each one with your students. Determine the levels of each criterion. Provide examples of each level so that students will have a visual representation of the expectations for the specific task.

(Serif Images)

- ***Provide a copy of the completed rubric for reference***: Students should have a completed copy of the rubric in order to monitor their progress during the assignment. A checklist involving the rubric can include a step-by-step list of "must haves" required for successful completion.
- ***Encourage self-evaluation using the rubric***: Allow students the opportunity to self-evaluate their work using the rubric prior to the formal teacher evaluation. Doing so will help students take personal responsibility for their work as well as demonstrate their understanding of the overall expectations for the task.

DON'T:

- ***Set final grades in stone***: Because it is important for students to view learning as an ongoing process, it is beneficial to allow students to make improvements to their assignment if they are not satisfied with the grade they earned. This allows students to learn from their mistakes and increases mastery.
- ***Forget about the rubric***: Teachers often spend countless hours developing and creating a rubric but it is useless if it is not referenced throughout the assignment. Think of a rubric as a teaching tool, not just a grading instrument. Use it as an important part of the learning process.

Kathy Galford

Rubric Websites for Teachers

There are many free, online resources available to help teachers develop their own rubrics for classroom use. These easily navagable sites offer tutorials and templates as well as access to hundreds of teacher-designed rubrics.

Among the best rubric websites are:

- **Rubrics4Teachers**: The Teacher Planet website provides dozens of easily adaptable rubrics sorted by subject matter and grade level.
- **Rubisar**: This free site allows teachers to create, edit, and store rubrics online.
- **iRubric**: There are over 360,000 rubrics available online at iRubric. Rubrics are searchable and can be downloaded at no charge to teachers.

Name _____   Date _____

Class _____   Period _____

		Criteria			Value
	4	**3**	**2**	**1**	
Ability to Focus	Always reads quietly the entire time; does not talk or interrupt others.	Usually reads quietly the entire time; tries not to talk or interrupt others.	Wanders around, reads a little; may talk and interrupt others on occasion.	Wanders around; talks, and interrupts others.	___
Activity Level	Takes a physically active part in game or activity all the time.	Takes a physically active part in game or activity most of the time.	Requires reminding daily to participate in game or activity.	Does not participate in game or activity.	___
Creativity	The student work demonstrates a unique level of originality.	The student work demonstrates originality.	The student's work lacked sincere originality.	The piece shows little or no evidence of original thought.	___
Eye Contact	Holds attention of entire audience with the use of direct eye contact.	Consistent use of direct eye contact with audience.	Displayed minimal eye contact with audience.	No eye contact is made with the audience.	___
Following Directions	Responds to teachers instruction without hesitation all the time.	Responds to teachers instruction without hesitation most of the time.	Responds to teachers instruction after non verbal cues are used.	Rarely responds to teachers instruction.	___
				Total:-----	___

TEACHER COMMENTS

Sample Social Studies Rubric available at the Teacher Planet website

How To Effectively Personalize Student Report Cards

Report cards are a powerful resource to communicate academic and behavioral progress to parents or guardians. It is imperative that teachers are clear and concise in providing an accurate description of student progress. Due to space limitations, though, comments have to be succinct, and these critical teacher assessments should be positive, meaningful, and personalized.

DO:

- *Always begin with a positive statement*: Although there are numerous items that you need to address with parents regarding their child's classroom behavior and performance, start your performance assessments with a sentence that praises the student. This will demonstrate your understanding of the child's strengths in the classroom setting and will set a positive tone for all subsequent communication that you will have throughout the school year.

- *Specify a reasonable goal*: Within your comments, set an academic or behavior goal for the student to achieve which will encourage their progress throughout the next reporting period. This will provide the avenue for an effective home-school connection by creating a positive parent partnership. It also enlists the parent as an active participant in their child's ongoing educational journey.

(Comstock Images)

50

- **_Encourage self-evaluation_**: Students need to be active participants in their own learning. Encouraging self-evaluation in the learning process fosters student ownership of decisions and empowers students to take responsibility for their progress. Prior to the issuing of every report card or progress report, teachers should conference with each of their students in order to set desirable goals for the next learning cycle. Students should be encouraged to create their own goals in conjunction with the teacher's recommendations.
- **_Keep all parties in the "loop"_**: It is essential that parents are consistently informed throughout all marking periods as to the progress students are making as well as areas that need improvement. Providing descriptive feedback on formative assessments, returning grades in a timely manner, and keeping open lines of communication with parents and guardians in terms of student development will prevent any unwanted "surprises" at the end of grading periods.

DON'T:

- **_Relay sensitive student information electronically_**: In our current digital age, teachers commonly rely upon electronic forms of communication. However, the convenience of electronic modes of communication can be perilous and should never be used to share sensitive or private information concerning students. All school divisions have explicit policies and procedures on the appropriate use of electronic communication. It is imperative that all teachers adhere to these policies and procedures and that they remember that all email contact is considered to be an official form of school communication.
- **_Be general_**: The purpose of a report card is to relay specific information about a student's academic development and progress. A generalized or vague statement about a student may be misinterpreted or even harmful. Keep your comments meaningful, specific, and individualized.
- **_Be repetitive_**: Each marking period needs to provide current goals and information for your students. Comments should reflect student progress and areas for improvement. As goals are set throughout the year, report card comments should not be repetitive since students are, hopefully, progressing towards achieving their goals. Remember to set new or revised goals each grading period so that students can move forward on their individualized continuum of learning.

Carolyn Lewis

Remember that all email is considered to be an official form of school communication!

Reflection on Teaching and Student Learning

Reflection is critical to effective instruction. Without the regular and active practice of reflection, teachers will never be truly successful in understanding how students actually learn, nor will they be able to target their teaching strengths and strategies to implement best practices for their students. Reflection is far more than asking, "How did that lesson go? or "Did my students 'get it?'" Serious reflection requires observations of student learning, the accurate documentation of student understanding, analysis of student work, and the use of data to guide instruction.

But reflection is not solely the teacher's responsibility. It must be an integral part of the learning process and should be modeled for students so they, too, will be able to reflect upon their work. Likewise, they need to be able to assess the progress they are making as well as their choices about their own learning. This can be achieved through descriptive feedback given by both their teachers and their peers. Reflection is a powerful approach to learning and should be an essential component of instruction.

DO:

- *Document notable observations*: Keep organized, anecdotal records and checklists on the performance of your students. Consult these notes frequently to determine student learning and needs in order to get the data necessary to adjust your lessons to ensure student progression in the learning process.
- *Analyze student work*: Assessing the details of student work is essential to understanding a student's individual process of moving from practice to product. By looking regularly and carefully at student work, you will be able to add to your data and this will support the decisions you make as you individualize instruction for academic growth. Whether it be flexible grouping, noticing misconceptions, or the need to reteach a concept in a different way, the analysis of student work can give you a "peek" into the brain processes of your students.
- *Use reflection as a mirror*: All types of reflection that you do as a teacher will inform the way you view yourself as the facilitator of learning. How do you question your students? How do you give directions? How do you set expectations? These are all a part of the self-reflection process and will give you the opportunity to see yourself as a learner as you continue to evolve and progress as an educator.

- *Give descriptive feedback*: When encouraging students to look at their own work, it is essential to give descriptive feedback. First, specify what they were successful with and then provide specific suggestions on how they can improve.
- *Encourage students to create individualized goals*: With your guidance, students will be able to see their strengths as well as their areas that need improvement. Conduct regular student conferences to access how students view themselves and their learning. In consultation with your students, create a goal sheet of items that you feel are attainable. This increases student responsibility and gives a sense of pride and independence with learning.

DON'T:

- *Neglect the importance of reflection in student learning*: Value the opportunity to incorporate the process of self and student reflection in your classroom. The benefits can be immeasurable and will allow you to reach your goals as a teacher. It will also enable you to better understand how your students learn and how you can plan for the most effective instruction.

Karen Drosinos

Things to do in:

- *March 2nd is Dr. Seuss' birthday! Make this day special by celebrating the importance of literacy.*
- *Begin to write personal notes to students to encourage them as they prepare for standardized testing.*
- *Begin to plan something special to do as you look forward to spring break.*
- *"Lucky to be me!" Have students reflect on what they feel fortunate to have.*
- *Take your students on a fun, content-rich field trip.*
- *Listen to "The Rite of Spring" by Igor Stravinsky on your way to school.*

TEACHER FILES

Beyond the Count:
Creative Grouping Strategies

"I'm going to count off; now each of you remember your number! One… two… three…"
It was the traditional teacher mantra for creating groups for classroom activities. Cooperative learning remains an important strategy for encouraging student learning and growth. There are, in fact, many ways of formulating groups. There are times when it is important to strategically place certain students into key roles to ensure the success of a lesson while there are other times when it is important to carefully balance personalities and academic abilities. It is essential that teachers utilize their professional judgment when determining the appropriate make up for groups. Variety is important and a random selection for organizing an activity forces students to develop interpersonal skills and to adapt to other learning styles.

Innovative Suggestions for Grouping Strategies

- *Playing Cards* can be used to create groups ranging from two to thirteen students. There are several variations with this technique:
    * The cards can be sorted by color (red/black) for two groups.
    * The cards can be organized by suit for two to four groups.
    * The cards can be sorted by face value for up to thirteen groups of four students each.

- *"Puzzle Pieces"* is a creative technique which can be used to create groups of any number and size. Before class, a teacher pre-cuts paper into a number of puzzle pieces based upon the number of students for each group. For example, if you would like groups of three students, you would cut each paper into three pieces. All of the pieces would be put into a bowl, and the students would randomly select a puzzle piece. Then, each student must match their

- her own piece with those of other students in order to complete their puzzle and formulate a group. To make this technique even more fun, you can use photographs, posters, seasonal items, or holiday cards.

- *Popsicle Sticks* can be used to create groups of any number or size. Numbers or pictures are placed on the end of each stick and then the students can draw popsicle sticks from a cup. The groups are formulated by students matching either their number or picture.

- *Grouping Cards* On her blog, teacher Laura Doran explains about her success using grouping cards to create small groups of two students. She makes small cards, often based upon a different season or holiday, and then distributes them to her students. For each category/season, there are 31 cards available (with one group of three for an odd-number of students). Each child receives a card and is instructed not to look at the card until told to do so. The students' job is to silently find their partner by looking for the person with the matching card. Teachers can find a free PDF and further explanation of this fun technique at: *http://laurabloggerclassroom.blogspot.com/2013/03/grouping-cards-free-for-your-classroom.html.*

(Comstock Images)

Teacher Erin Ford has created a variation of the grouping card technique. Each card has a number, a shape, an ice cream flavor, an animal, and a school supply. Erin suggests creating the cards on different colored paper and laminating them. Each of the six categories (including card color) can be used to create a different group. The best part of this method is that the students are choosing a card without any knowledge of the grouping category. Only later will the teacher reveal whether the new groups will be formulated by numbers, shapes, ice cream flavors, animals, school supplies, or card color. Students truly enjoy this grouping strategy because it contains an element of surprise. Additional information is available at Erin's website along with detailed instructions as well as a free download: *https://sites.google.com/site/mrsfordsenglishclasses/Home/ideas-for-teachers/grouping-cards*.

Tabitha Strickler

REMEMBER

1. All grouping strategies require pre-planning. Not only do you need to create the materials for your chosen technique, but you also need to know how many students are present for the activity.
2. Laminating materials allows you to reuse your materials for years.

(Serif Premium Images)

Chapter IV

"Forging Parent Partnerships & Community Connections"

(Comstock Images)

Making a Difference Together: The Power of Effective Parent-Teacher Communication

A challenge for all teachers is learning to communicate effectively with parents in such a way that by the end of each conversation everyone is on the same team and committed to a common goal. The approach taken with parents does matter. Get it right, and you have a strong ally for the year, increasing the chances of the student persevering through challenges and thriving. Get it wrong, and you lose the parent's respect and support, decreasing the chances of the student making needed strides.

Consider the following African proverb as you craft the approach that best fosters a student's growth academically, emotionally, and socially: "If you want to go fast, go alone. If you want to go far, go together." Invest the time and establish productive partnerships with parents early on so that students have a cohesive team coaching and cheering them on throughout the year long journey. Remember, it is all about the students and sometimes they need a team approach to thrive.

DO:

- *Be available and approachable*: It is important to set a welcoming tone at the beginning of the year. Parents are more inclined to work with you if they feel like a valued partner in their child's education. Carefully craft your initial written and verbal communication to stress collaboration between home and school. Be flexible in your availability to conference instead of rigid, and try to connect to your parents when conveying your passion for teaching and reaching all students. It may be necessary to secure a translator for parents who do not speak English as a first language.
- *Know your students*: Make it a priority to find ways to connect with all students. Learn about their interests, celebrate their successes, and let them know that you care about them. Stay in tune with their progress and struggles. Knowing your students and having a positive relationship with them will pay off tremendously when communicating with parents. Whether you or a parent has a concern to share, the parent needs to have some indication that you "know" their child. Let a parent know you have a vested interest in their child.

- ***Provide timely feedback***: In the age of instant access to information, parents and students are accustomed to obtaining information quickly. This needs to be considered when grading papers, returning papers, and updating gradebooks. Feedback on student performance needs to be timely because when too much time has transpired, students and parents lose interest and any positive correction becomes less likely. If your school posts grades for online parent access, establish a routine of uploading current grades weekly. Be timely, and help a parent have an on-going pulse of their child's performance.

- ***Reach out early***: Regardless of the grade or subject you teach, when you have a concern regarding a student, don't be afraid to reach out to parents. Parents appreciate a proactive teacher and are more willing to support and offer insight when approached early.

- ***Listen and try to understand different perspectives***: There will be times when parents contact you to express concerns. When these are directed towards you, it can be intimidating and can make it difficult to continue a positive dialogue. You should try not to take criticism personally since much can be gleaned by listening and trying to understand a different perspective. There will be times when a resolution can be easily brainstormed and implemented to everyone's satisfaction. Sometimes, however, there will not be an obvious resolution and this is where it will be very important to make sure that the parents are courteously heard and their opinions respected.

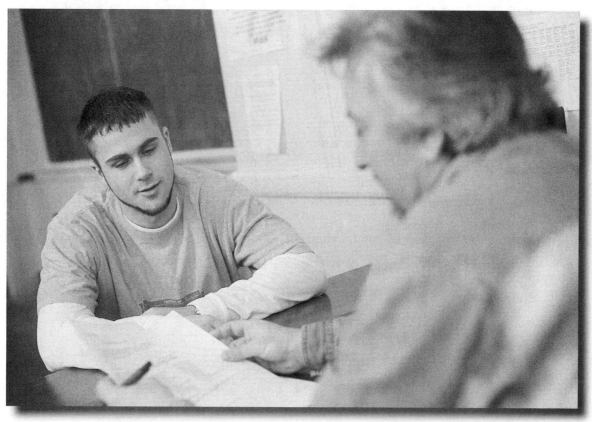

(Corbis Images)

- **Seek support**: If at any time you feel uncomfortable in meeting with a parent or you are unsure about how to respond, seek out your administrator or school counselor for advice. They are trained to provide guidance on how to best craft your conversations with parents. If you are still uncomfortable, request that your administrator join the conference. This approach diffuses potentially negative situations more quickly.

DON'T:

- **Ignore a parent**: Despite how busy you may be, always make time to respond to parents in a timely manner. A good rule to follow is to respond within twenty-four hours.
- **Attack or be defensive**: Remember that parents are entrusting their child to you, so you need to be approachable. Regardless of the tone of a given conversation, always maintain your composure and remain calm. Becoming aggressive is unproductive and unprofessional. It is better to terminate a conference prematurely than to further exacerbate a delicate situation. Take time to reflect on what was transpired and follow up with another conversation. This should help the next meeting go more smoothly. Remember, alert your administrator when you have had a tough encounter, and you must be open to suggestions and additional support.
- **Surprise a parent**: Always be upfront with parents. When scheduling conferences, make sure to inform parents if others will be joining you during that time. Don't let the report card be the first time that the parents learn that their child is struggling in class. Lack of communication will quickly damage your ongoing relationship with parents. Always be honest and timely.
- **Rely on electronic communication**: Although e-mail is the quickest and most convenient way to contact a parent, it can also be the source of numerous problems. While e-mail can be effective in sharing routine information like assignments, upcoming assessments, and school activities, refrain from using it to share confidential matters or to respond to serious concerns. Remember, e-mail and text messaging are frequently subject to misinterpretation, and it can be easily shared and transmitted to others. All correspondence is considered to be an official communication from the school, so the best way to ensure effective communication is to have a traditional phone conversation or parent conference.

Raegan Rangel

Ten Inspirational Teacher Movies

- *Mr. Holland's Opus* (1995) starring Richard Dreyfuss
- *Stand and Deliver* (1988) starring Edward James Olmos
- *Conrack* (1974) starring Jon Voight
- *Remember the Titans* (2000) starring Danzel Washington
- *Dead Poets Society* (1989) starring Robin Williams
- *Lean on Me* (1989) starring Morgan Freeman
- *The Emperor's Club* (2002) starring Kevin Kline
- *The Prime of Miss Jean Brody* (1969) starring Maggie Smith
- *To Sir, with Love* (1967) starring Sidney Poitier
- *Freedom Writers* (2007) starring Hilary Swank

Parent Conferences: Forging Partnerships

(Elementary)

Parent conferences provide important opportunities to forge partnerships and to continue these learning conversations. The preparation for such face-to-face interaction is critical since the meetings serve as an avenue to communicate student progress and to build relationships with parents. Even though some parents may prefer to conference via phone, such teacher-parent contact requires specialized preparation and your focused attention.

DO:

- *Plan ahead*: Days set aside for parent conferences are hectic and exhausting. Teachers will have little downtime between conferences, so it is essential to be ready and well-prepared for each conference. Organization is the key. You should have pre-prepared copies of all assessment data, grade sheets, student portfolios, and other relevant material for the parents. This will save valuable time and focus your conversations during each of the conferences.

- *Listen*: Often, teachers are too anxious to dispense information during a parent conference and may unintentionally fail to listen. You should always act as a facilitator of the discussion by asking questions and probing for information. By allowing parents the time to voice their concerns and to ask questions, you will receive much pertinent information about their child.

- *Stay focused*: Parent conferences are often limited to a set period of time. Usually this is no more than 10 or 20 minutes in duration. Therefore, teachers need to stay on topic during each appointment in order to respect the parents' time. Avoid wasting time with superfluous and meaningless conversation. Staying focused is essential in conducting an effective and productive conference.

- *Encourage continued and future communication*: Conferences should not end the conversation but should establish the basis for opening channels of continuing conversations between teachers and parents. Keeping lines of communication open throughout the school year is critical to student success. Frequent phone calls, newsletters, classroom websites, and other teacher outreach are ways teachers can continue their active partnerships with parents.

DON'T:

- *Use educational jargon*: Teachers need to remember that parents may not be familiar with so-called "teacher talk." Make a conscious effort to avoid the use of acronyms or other educational terms that may be confusing and unhelpful. Being proactive in this regard will strengthen your relationships with parents and will help elicit their support in your efforts to help their child's academic progress.
- *Take conferences casually*: Remember that although parent conference day is typically a day "without" students, it is a day expressly designed to help students. The impression that you make will influence the perception parents will have of you and of your school. You are a representative of the teaching profession and you need to take this responsibility very seriously by conducting yourself in a manner that reflects the dignity of the profession. Your demeanor, dress, and conduct will set the tone for the conference and will impact the parents' perceptions of the profession.
- *Make student comparisons*: During conferences, it is important to focus the time and discussion on topics directly related to the individual student. Never make comparisons to peers or siblings. There is a lot of pertinent information that you need to share with parents and your conference time provides you an important opportunity to demonstrate your desire to help as well as your concern for their child.

Carolyn Lewis

Things to do in:

- *It's Spring Cleaning time! Organize your files and begin to purge unused materials.*
- *Remember to do your taxes and use your teacher credit.*
- *Commemorate Arbor Day by planting a tree in your school community.*
- *April 22nd is Earth Day. Challenge your students to create something from recycled materials.*

Parent Conferences
(Secondary)

After your first few weeks of school, you will be comfortable standing in front of the class and delivering instruction. Your first official parent conference can be an daunting experience. However, remember that these meetings are a critical communication tool, and it is important to make the most of them. Parents are your greatest allies, and there are several things that you can do to make such meetings more comfortable and productive for everyone involved.

DO:

- *Plan to make a good first impression*: Parents will be visiting your classroom for the first time. They will logically draw conclusions from their first impressions about your organization, structure, and your competence as a teacher. Your room doesn't have to look perfect or antiseptic, but it is important that you clean up in advance any unnecessary mess or clutter.
- *Make parents comfortable*: Always greet parents with a friendly "hello" and invite them into your room. Have a small table available with a few chairs around it. Be sure to locate chairs that are comfortable for adults.
- *Dress professionally and appropriately*: You should always dress tastefully and modestly while in school. If you teach a subject that requires durable clothing such as in science, career technical education, or physical education, wear a lab coat, smock, or clothing which displays the school's logo.
- *Prepare*: Before the meeting, be sure to print off all relevant grade reports and assignments that you wish to discuss with parents. Think seriously about the involved student and prepare a list of positive comments and traits. Consider where the child can improve and be prepared to discuss any concerns. Always do this in a positive manner. Your primary goal is to help the child be successful in your class.
- *Keep the meeting focused, positive, and productive*: Keep small talk to a minimum. You do not want to waste people's time with irrelevant conversation. Keep the focus on the student especially his academic progress. Listen carefully to what parents have to say, particularly about any home issues that could be impacting a child's academic performance.

DON'T:

- **Surprise parents**: All grades should have been shared with the student and the parents prior to the meeting. If there are concerns you want to address, make sure they are known prior to the conference.

- **Have unscheduled conferences outside of school**: Remember that all students' grades and performance are confidential. Any discussions with parents should be confined to a formal setting with a school counselor or administrator present. Do not discuss a child's performance outside of the school setting or at extracurricular activities. If parents ask outside of school, compliment their child, but request that the parents schedule a formal conference.

- **Forget the time frame**: Always be punctual for a conference and start on time. In cases where there is a specified time interval set aside for individual sessions such as on a conference day, use a visual clock or timer so that you can keep to your schedule. Don't keep others waiting in line to see you.

- **Discuss other students**: The focus of the conference should always remain on the parent's child and should not involve discussions of other students in the class.

Susanne Dana

Did you listen?

Did you share what was important?

Did you comment on the student's strengths?

Did you and the parent agree on a plan, if necessary?

Did you thank the parent for coming in?

Things to do in:

- *Invite your principal to co-teach a lesson in your classroom.*
- *Have an ice cream social for your students prior to high-stakes testing.*
- *Thank a colleague that you respect.*
- *Commemorate Memorial Day by teaching a lesson on its historic significance.*
- *Start collecting boxes for summer room preparations.*

MAY

Creating Learning Bridges through Community Service

The classroom is the traditional hub of student learning but there are also numerous opportunities outside the confines of the classroom walls or even the school building. There are many possibilities for the local community to become involved in the learning process of your students. It is important to have the public interact with the schools and the curriculum that we are teaching. Through donations, volunteerism, and community partnerships, teachers can expand their outreach and enlist new partners in the educational process.

Much of what we teach needs to be applied to real-world situations. By creating experiences for students to participate in their own community, we help expand student knowledge and develop a sense of civic responsibility. Community service should be considered a bridge of learning. Community members and citizens can be encouraged to become involved in the classroom while students can give back to their community through appropriate service projects. This bridge of learning is a two-way street and demonstrates the power that students have in making a positive difference in their own backyards.

DO:

- ***Invite community members into your classroom***: There are many members in the community (firefighters, law enforcement, health professionals, military) who are willing to volunteer in your classroom. These community members not only reinforce the importance of learning, but also serve as role models for students by establishing and maintaining constructive relationships with them. You can get in contact with these individuals with a phone call, e-mail, or letter. If you reach out to the community, you will find an abundance of interest and support.
- ***Plan accordingly***: You should speak to your administrator prior to making any contact with non-school employees. Principals need to know who will be entering their building and why. It is important to follow carefully the volunteer guidelines mandated by your individual school district. Potential volunteers will be required to fill out specified paperwork and may be expected to attend mandated training for volunteers as well as have a background check conducted by local law enforcement agencies. For the safety of your students and school, it is imperative that you make all of these arrangements prior to enlisting school volunteers.

- ***Initiate community service through student decision making***: Involve students when establishing a community service project. Use brainstorming techniques to discuss which organizations might benefit from their involvement. Then, facilitate discussions as to what type of service would be most beneficial. For example, students in a large military-populated school district might decide to send holiday cards to deployed Navy ships. When students become the decision makers in community service, they will take ownership and responsibility. This will have the benefit of turning a learning experience into a life-changing lesson.

DON'T:

- ***Hesitate to reach out to community businesses***: Local businesses are often interested and willing to become involved in supporting student learning and school-directed initiatives. Solicit specific materials or donations for specific projects. Once again, remember to check with your administrator concerning your school's guidelines and policies relating to donations and contributions.
- ***Forget to thank each community partnership for their involvements in your classroom***: It is important to show gratitude for the support and involvement of the community. This demonstrates good manners and it will foster positive partnerships for the future. Have the students write individual thank you notes, and express your appreciation publicly in your classroom and school newsletters. This adds a personal touch and shows your community partners that their involvement in your classroom and school was truly appreciated and valued.

Karen Drosinos

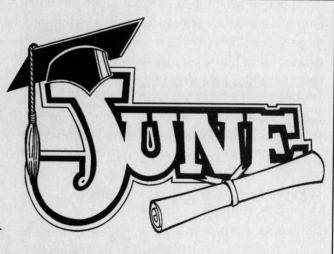

Things to do in:

- *Thank your students for a wonderful year by writing an individual message to each.*
- *The year is not over yet. Continue to teach until the last day and make learning fun!*
- *Commemorate the year by organizing a student and family gathering.*
- *Reflect on your successes this school year.*
- *Attend commencement exercises for the high school in your area.*

Making the Connection Between Home and School

Effective communication with parents and students is an important responsibility of all teachers. We sometimes take for granted that we communicate with our students in the classroom but it is also important that we reach out regularly to parents and guardians. By sharing critical information in an efficient and timely manner, a school becomes a more welcoming and inclusive place while helping teachers create a strong supportive network to foster learning.

Most elementary teachers routinely provide parents with a printed newsletter which details the "happenings" of the school week or month. Secondary teachers often communicate the same information to parental groups through email messages. While these methods of communication are effective, modern technology has made digital forms of communication more accessible and such information is now easier to disseminate. Using such technological resources allow parents and students immediate access to critical updates, assignments, news, and files at any time.

Today, all educators should maintain a current class website to support their instruction. New, up-to-date software and templates make creating high quality, informative websites easy. It is no longer necessary to have an in-depth understanding of complex html coding.

What to Include in a Class Websites

- *A Home Page*: This initial page should be graphically appealing and welcome visitors to your site. It should detail the purpose of your website and have readily accessible connecting links to the school's main page, the school superintendent and division, as well as the state department of education. Keep your opening home page concise and clutter-free. Use a navigation bar to link to specific content areas.

- ***Contact/Biographical Information***: This page should provide parents and students with detailed information about how to best contact the teacher, including email and the school phone number. It is also appropriate to provide some background information including colleges, degrees, certifications, professional associations, and related information. If you desire, you can also provide some information about your interests and hobbies. However, do not share any private, personal, or family information.

- ***Content Pages***: These linked pages should focus on each subject or preparation that a teachers has. For example, an English teacher may have separate pages for AP English and English 10. This provides parents and students with more direction on where to find information that is applicable to them. Class-specific assignments and deadlines should be shared on these pages.

- ***Extra-curricular Activities***: Separate pages should be focused on clubs, sports, or activities that a teacher sponsors or coaches. An online calendar with practice schedules, game dates and times, club meetings, or special events is exceedingly helpful for both students and parents.

Tabitha Strickler

Be familiar with your school division's policies regulating social media. Never share or post your personal and private social media profiles to professional websites, blogs, or email signatures. Some teachers may wish to create specific Facebook pages or Twitter feeds exclusively for their classes or clubs, but there may be specific policies that prohibit such communication between teachers and students. It is always wise to err on the side of caution.

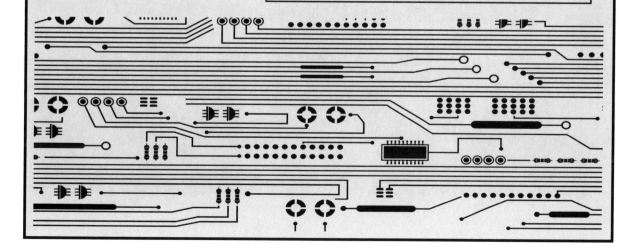

Google Sites is a great resource for teachers. It provides free website templates plus online storage. It also has the following valuable resources:

- *Announcements*: a site that acts much like a blog with most recent posts being posted on top
- *File Cabinet*: a place to upload and manage linked documents from a computer
- *List Page*: a location to add and track lists of information

sites.google.com

What about Blogs?

A blog is a type of website that is frequently updated, interactive, and features a running catalog of posts. Each post can consist of relatively small portions of information, links, images, or video and are shown in reverse chronological order with the most recent material at the top of the page. Many blogs perform as an online diary. Blogs are often more dynamic than websites, with more constant updates, links, and the possibilities for interaction between blogger and audience. Security features are frequently available that allow bloggers the ability to limit who can read and/or contribute to the blog. Two other common features of a blog are a post archive and the ability of readers to make comments on posts.

(Media Focus LLD)

Chapter V

"Professionalism 101"

(Comstock Images)

Finding Your "Soul Mate" in Your Building

As social beings, teachers often seek out colleagues with common interests in hopes of building professional and personal relationships within their workplace. A school is not only a place of learning but it is also a hub of socialization for both students and faculty alike. Teachers naturally want to commiserate with their colleagues and to share their triumphs, challenges, passions, and frustrations. Yet who you choose to surround yourself with can have a dramatic effect on your overall attitude and perception. Therefore, it is critical that you make wise choices in seeking and selecting your professional "soul mate."

DO:

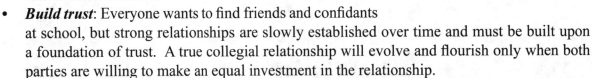

Always Associate with Positive People

- **Seek out positive, realistic people**: A person's outlook will inevitably influence another's for better or for worse. For this reason, teachers need to find people in their buildings who are positive and aware of the daily realities of classroom teaching. Positive, realistic teachers do not see the world through "rose colored" glasses, but understand the challenges they face and strive to do their best, regardless of circumstances.
- **Build trust**: Everyone wants to find friends and confidants at school, but strong relationships are slowly established over time and must be built upon a foundation of trust. A true collegial relationship will evolve and flourish only when both parties are willing to make an equal investment in the relationship.
- **Share respectfully**: It is important that you can freely and openly share your thoughts, challenges, frustrations, successes, and triumphs. Still, it is critical you remain professional when speaking with colleagues. As a member of a team, always share respectfully so that you can build lasting, trusting relationships.

DON'T:

- ***Gravitate to the "negative Nancys" in your building***: Negative people destroy morale and the goodness around them often because of their own personal inadequacies and unhappiness. This creates a negative undercurrent in schools and discounts the core purpose of the teaching profession: educating students and looking after their well-being. It is imperative that you steer clear of those individuals who partake in gossip, complain, and defame their fellow teachers. Negative teachers are detrimental to your professional development and are the bane of administrators. Associating with such people will demean you as a professional.

- ***Be afraid to reach out to a colleague***: As a new teacher, it is initially difficult to integrate and fit in at your school. Never be afraid to take the first step in building a collegial relationship. Initiate conversations with your colleagues and offer to assist with tasks and take on new responsibilities. Taking these first steps will forge professional relationships within your building and can open doors for truly lasting and satisfying friendships.

- ***Sweep problems under the rug***: When problems arise, it is important that they are handled in a professional manner. Most issues stem from ineffective communication. Make sure that you actively listen to your fellow teachers and give them your respect. Pay attention to what they are saying instead of trying to think of a response while they are speaking. It is always helpful to restate to them your understanding about their comments or requests. This will eliminate many of the issues that arise from miscommunications.

Stephanie Doyle

Things to do in:

- *Take a vacation with family or friends to relax and enjoy warm weather.*
- *Celebrate the 4th of July with a picnic and fireworks.*
- *Enroll in a summer workshop or seminar.*
- *Read a novel for enjoyment.*
- *Visit a National Park.*
- *Write a long, handwritten letter to an old friend.*
- *Take a "week off" from all email, cell phones, and social media.*
- *Get some exercise.*
- *Have FUN!*

Connecting with Colleagues

Some teachers are considered to be foxhole educators. They close their doors, teach their classes, and refuse to participate in school activities. To be a truly professional educator, though, you not only have to be a good classroom teacher, you need to be a good colleague. A school is a collection of a diverse group of people all working together as a team to educate children. You will need to share resources and materials, develop a common curriculum, and possibly even co-teach classes.

DO:

- *Respect the school's culture*: All schools have their own unique philosophy and culture. It is important that you learn and respect it. You need to know proper procedures, which can vary widely from school to school and even between departments.
- *Seek help*: When you need help or advice, always ask a colleague for help or suggestions.
- *Be Friendly*: Respect, support, and connect with other teachers by being friendly and accessible.
- *Accept differences*: All teachers have diverse teaching methods and educational philosophies. It is important that you honor and accept these differences.

(Comstock Images)

DON'T:

- ***Have a negative attitude***: Don't complain or criticize without knowing the facts. There are usually good reasons behind all school policies and procedures. Never engage in gossip about your fellow teachers or engage in public criticism of students. This is not only unbecoming, it is unprofessional.
- ***Bring personal problems to school***: The personal details of your life are private and should not adversely impact your teaching or your professional relationships.

Susanne Dana

Inspirational Quotes about Teachers and Teaching

- *"Teachers are more than any other class the guardians of civilization."* Bertrand Russell
- *"Teachers, I believe, are the most responsible and important members of society because their professional efforts affect the fate of the earth."* Helen Caldicott
- *"There's no word in the language I revere more than 'teacher.' My heart sings when a kid refers to me as his teacher, and it always has. I've honored myself and the entire family of man by becoming a teacher."* Pat Conroy
- *"The object of teaching a child is to enable him to get along without a teacher."* Elbert Hubbard
- *"Good teaching is more a giving of right questions than a giving of right answers."* Josef Albers
- *"A teacher affects eternity; he can never tell where his influence stops."* Henry Adams
- *"If we work upon marble, it will perish; if we work on brass, time will efface it. If we rear temples, they will crumble to dust. But if we work on men's immortal minds...we engrave on those tablets something which no time can efface, and which will brighten to all eternity."* Daniel Webster
- *"I have come to believe that a great teacher is a great artist and that there are as few as there are any other great artists. Teaching might even be the greatest of the arts since the medium is the human mind and spirit."* John Steinbeck

Getting the Most from Classroom Observations

Classroom observations can be intimidating for even the most experienced teachers. We want our administrators and colleagues to recognize that we are dedicated, effective, and competent, motivating, and inspiring our students to learn on a daily basis. Great teachers are always well-prepared for class and have detailed daily lesson plans. These are fundamental competencies and are essential in ensuring that you are poised and confident on evaluation days. Still, the reality of having an observer in the classroom monitoring your every move is daunting and we fear that we are going to be exposed as mere mortals with human flaws and frailties.

Remember that classroom observations are not punitive exercises; they are a positive opportunity to get important feedback that will help you improve as a teacher. Your administrator is an ally, not an enemy. The vast majority of school principals were once accomplished classroom teachers and they want their faculty to be successful. They view their teachers as the most important element in a school's overall success and in a positive educational environment. So, you should meet regularly with your subject area or grade level administrator to discuss expectations and to seek feedback. This proactive approach establishes a constructive dialogue that ensures that classroom visits will be a positive experience.

Read Andrew Rotherham's fascinating article, "Super Bowl School: What the NFL Can Teach Teachers," in *Time* magazine where he interviews two brothers (one an educational reformer and the other a teacher turned professional football coach) about feedback and evaluation in their respective fields.

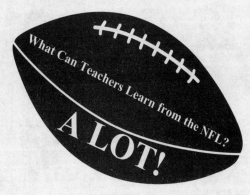

"In education, we've conditioned people to see feedback as a negative. In the NFL, they welcome it."

-Tim Daly

DO:

- *Prepare*: The anxiety that naturally stems from an observation can cause you to move too quickly through activities and course material. Just in case your pacing is off, have an additional class activity ready. The students will predictably fill any free time with their own antics and most classroom discipline problems occur within the first or last five minutes of class. Consider putting together a set of index cards with ideas for short activities or drills that can be used for additional instructional time. Ask your colleagues for their tricks as well. These ideas can be indispensable on days when your lesson progresses quicker than you anticipated.
- *Inform your class when an observer is coming*: Students may be apprehensive or intimidated with another adult's presence in their classroom. Whenever possible, let them know when a visitor is expected. Explain that the administrator is there to help everyone learn better.
- *Dress professionally, but comfortably*: All teachers should be able to move freely and quickly throughout the classroom. Remember that proximity is the best management tool. Dress appropriately, and wear clothing and shoes that allow you to move easily throughout the classroom. If you are uncomfortable in your new suit or high heels, you won't be able to focus on your instruction or on your students.

DON'T:

- *Try to impress*: Your administrator doesn't expect to observe all of the amazing things you can do in a single observation. Avoid trying out new or unusual instructional strategies for the first time. Avoid trying to cover too much content in a short time. As much as possible, be natural and conduct your lesson just like you do every other day. Be genuine and teach authentically with your students' best interests at heart.
- *Go outside of your comfort zone*: Every teacher has certain types of instructional activities that they prefer and which are compatible with their teaching style. Use these during observations. For example, if you enjoy working with small groups of students, plan to use this type of activity during your observation. Of course, all teachers should always be willing to try new, innovative instructional strategies and methods but this is not the time to experiment. Instead, go with the "tried and true" activities in which you are confident.
- *Get defensive*: Administrators will always mention areas where you can improve. Accept their critique as helpful feedback rather than a sign of disapproval. Even though you are personally vested in your lesson plans, they can always be improved. No one is perfect, and there is always room for improvement. Remember that the essence of teaching is determining how to best help your students learn and grow.

Susan Catlett

How To Be a Tech-Savvy Teacher

Technology is ever-changing. Constant upgrades and improvements to technology move the competitive market forward, which keeps consumers wanting to know more. This concept parallels the field of education, as your profession is one that is constantly evolving. It is necessary for you to keep current on your understanding of how technology can contribute to the effectiveness of your instruction, as well as student engagement.

Over the past decades, there has been an influx of technological ideas which have thrust their way into the American classroom. Educators have been inundated with software and hardware that have had a dramatic impact on student learning and have advanced teaching strategies. In addition to the overall benefits of integrating technology, its utilization will allow you to more efficiently record assessments, more effectively analyze data, and expand your ability to create engaging learning opportunities.

DO:

- ***Get to know the technology gurus in your building***: Within your building, there are people who are considered the technology "experts." These people are typically the media specialist and computer resource teacher. You will need to become familiar with these individuals so that you can freely and comfortably ask for assistance when incorporating new technology into your classroom. These professionals are also a great resource for you to build lessons and learning opportunities around the available technology in your school building.

- ***Participate in technology-related professional development***: Often, professional learning opportunities dealing with technology integration are offered within your school district or through local colleges and universities. These are invaluable workshops that can offer training and enhance your technology repertoire. An added bonus is that many of these workshops are chances to earn college credit or licensure renewal points. You will also receive new ideas to share with fellow colleagues at your school, as well as network and collaborate with educators who share a common interest in enhancing instruction with technology.

- ***Try, try again***: With all new things, success usually does not occur with the first attempt. However, do not be discouraged. Effective use of any tool takes time and practice. It will be important to explore each new piece of technology and increase your confidence in its usage over time. This will allow you the skill set to demonstrate the options technology has to offer to your students and to effectively incorporate it into instruction.

(Media Focus)

- ***Challenge your students to get in the technology "driver's seat"*** : Students today are technology natives and probably know more than you do. As more advancements are made, students are exposed at younger ages to technology. Consequently, children have a heightened comfort level with trying the latest gadgets on the market. Take advantage of your students' enthusiasm and interest in technology by encouraging them to teach you and their classmates. Make available to your students all that your school has to offer. In addition, check with your school division's policies and procedures about bringing personal devices to school.

- ***Manage appropriate use of technology***: Because many students are familiar with a variety of technology, the responsibility they demonstrate may be less than what you desire. It is critical to manage appropriate use of all devices. Assign each student a number that corresponds to a particular device. This will increase the accountability of care in using technology. You may also want to include safety procedures when accessing programs and using technology for research purposes.

DON'T:

- ***Leave technological devices unattended***: Despite the availability and affordability of technology, there remain individuals who may take personal advantage of the school setting and remove technology without permission. It is critical that you follow your school's mandated procedures for storing devices during and after school hours. Using technology costs money, and school budgets are already tight. Be mindful of this when using technology in your classroom.

- ***Stress***: It's not how much you use. It is how well you use it. The amount of technology that a school has to offer for teacher or student use can be overwhelming. It is important for you to select technology that is most appropriate to your instructional needs. Over time, you will find ways to incorporate a variety of instructional devices. However, do not feel as if you need to juggle numerous pieces of technology. Rather, focus on using single technology devices until your comfort level increases and you are ready to add another piece of technology to your instruction.

- ***Let budgets limit you***: It is important to acknowledge that school budgets may limit the amount of technology available to your school. Recent cuts have driven administrators to dial back purchases. Although the use of technology in the classroom is on the rise, the purchase of technology is determined by the availability of funds. Luckily, there are other ways that teachers can purchase technology for their classroom. Websites, such as Donorschoose. org, afford teachers purchasing opportunities that they might not otherwise receive. By writing a simple description of your classroom and your needs, public donors can select your classroom and fund your requests. To explore this option, you may want to visit www. donorschoose.org for more information.

- *Make excuses*: Everyone is busy and has a variety of tasks to accomplish in the day to day rigor of your profession. Sometimes it is easy to neglect certain tasks simply due to the amount of effort it takes in tackling something new. You need to avoid this temptation and forge ahead with your goals of incorporating new technology into your instructional day. This will have an enormous impact on your students and enhance your ability to implement new strategies involving technology in your classroom. Your efforts will be rewarded by the outcome of your students' success.

Stephanie Doyle and Karen Drosinos

Why I Teach!
Karen Drosinos

I remember myself as a first grader engaged in a lesson on making a mosaic butterfly. I was focused on cutting out perfectly colored squares to glue into my outlined shape, but before I knew it, it was time to stop and clean up. As we transitioned back to instruction, my teacher walked over to me with my mosaic butterfly and asked me if I wanted to continue working on my masterpiece, explaining to me that she was proud of my effort and creativity and was excited to see the completed product. My teacher continued with the lessons for that day, but I continued to work on my butterfly.

It is not the butterfly that I created that I remember most. Rather, what impacted me most was the way my teacher understood and valued how I learned. This is both the science and the art of teaching. I look forward with anticipation to the moment when a student makes a connection, to when a connection leads to higher- order thinking, and most importantly to the moment when I see that they love learning. My purpose as a teacher is to embed in each of my students the moment where they, too, believe that they can accomplish anything. Because, like my teacher believed in me, I, too, believe in each of them. My philosophy of teaching is simple: teaching is both a science and an art. The science of teaching is in understanding how children learn; the art of teaching lies in how you teach them.

And it is an outstanding teacher who can do just that.

(Philip Bigler)

Looking Out For #1

Teaching is a rewarding and exciting career. Every day, you are challenged. You think, talk, listen, entertain, cajole, encourage, question, read, write, laugh, and correct--often within a short class period. Even when your careful planning and activities go flawlessly, good teachers go home exhausted. Still, you must grade papers and prepare for the next day. Your students are deserving of your best efforts each and every day.

The truth is that teachers are not allowed to have very many bad days. We must leave our personal baggage and problems at home, because our students have to be our primary concern at school. To be at your best, you need to take care of yourself physically and emotionally. You have to work to develop a positive, optimistic attitude which will ensure a long and productive teaching career.

(Comstock Images)

DO:

> *"To be at your best, you need to take care of yourself physically and emotionally."*

- *Get enough sleep*: Everyone knows how important adequate sleep is to be productive and intellectually alert. Go to bed at a reasonable hour and get at least eight hours of sleep. If you are consistently tired—physically, emotionally, psychologically—you will not be an effective teacher.
- *Eat breakfast*: The positive effects of eating breakfast on cognitive function have been well documented through research. Problem-solving skills, verbal fluency, and memory all suffer when you skip breakfast. Be sure to give your brain some fuel to work with before you get to school.

- *Eat lunch with positive friends and colleagues*: A 30-minute stress-free and relaxing lunch with other teachers is rejuvenating. It gives you a chance to debrief, share ideas, get help, and develop friendships. You will always need trustworthy colleagues who you can depend upon and these relationships are often cultivated in the faculty lunch room. Avoid the negative teachers, the "lounge lizards," who poison the school's environment with their constant complaints and incessant gossip.

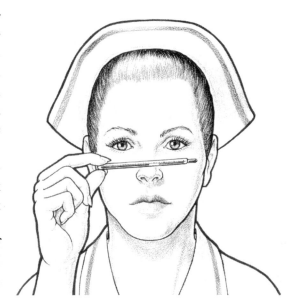

- *Use your sick days when ill*: It takes a lot of time and effort to put together a good substitute plan, but it is worth it when you are sick or not feeling well. You should not feel guilty about being absent when you are truly sick; your students will be able to survive without you for a day, and it is important that you avoid spreading your illness to others. Try exchanging a set of prepared substitute plans with other teachers and have them ready in the case of an emergency absence.

- *Do something just for yourself*: Teaching is a high pressure job, and it is important to embrace a healthy lifestyle as a way to deal with the resulting stress. Find activities that you love and make them a regular part of your routine. These could include such things as exercise, reading, meditating, cooking, relaxing with friends, getting a massage, or taking a luxurious afternoon nap. Whatever it is that brings you peace and joy, reserve time for it.

DON'T:

- *Stay too late at school*: All teachers will occasionally have to stay late at school in order to prepare for a special lesson or to fulfill school responsibilities. But after a long day of working with students, you need to go home and spend time with the people you love. You will be far more productive by arriving a little earlier at school the next day, refreshed and renewed.

- *Work on Sundays*: An old axiom asserts that a teacher's work is never done, but you should always designate one day per week as your day off from school work. This is a time to focus on other things and will help you be more energetic on work days.

- *Say yes to every request*: Effective teachers are routinely asked to serve on committees, lead workshops, coach teams, chaperone clubs, and sponsor school activities. It is okay to say "no" once in a while. You must set strict limits on your time or you will find yourself overwhelmed and frustrated in a very short period of time. Agree to only the things that you are passionate about.

Susan Catlett

It's OK to Say "NO"

As a teacher, you have many professional responsibilities and duties. Each day, you are expected to prepare and deliver quality instruction and assessment and this is your primary obligation. This alone can be overwhelming and during your early career, you may not be ready to assume additional duties or to take on the numerous other things that administrators, parents, and students may request of you such as coaching responsibilities, extra-curricular activities, club sponsorships, and weekend activities. It is important for you to know when and how to say "no" appropriately in order to maximize your effectiveness as a classroom teacher as well as to maintain your sanity. Still, you need to participate in school functions and avoid being perceived as uninvolved-while keeping your focus on your students.

DO:

- *Recognize that a school is a complex organization*: It takes much more than just good teaching to make a school run efficiently and effectively. Teachers should make every effort to participate in non-instructional activities.
- *Carefully listen and evaluate requests*: Make sure that if you decide to refuse something, there is a valid reason, rather than as an excuse to avoid additional work. Your primary responsibility is your students.
- *Differentiate with reason*: Always distinguish between a one-time request due to extenuating circumstances and an unreasonable assignment. There will be times when you need to be flexible and balance a variety of duties as circumstances may occur during the course of a school day. However, it will be imperative to use your professional judgment when requests from colleagues, administrators, or parents arise that are questionable.
- *Say "yes" if you can*: Understand that working with students, parents, and colleagues outside of the classroom can foster positive relationships and can be a rewarding experience.

(Comstock Images)

DON'T:

- *Become defensive*: It is important to calmly discuss all situations as a professional. If you find you cannot do what is being asked or if the request is unreasonable, explain your reasons honestly.

- *Question people's motives*: Remember that the person who is seeking your assistance has a legitimate need or is facing a problem that needs resolution. Even if you have to say no, you can still be supportive in contributing to a solution.

- *Overextend yourself*: You cannot please everyone all of the time. Your first priority must be your students. Extracurricular responsibilites should never take precedence over your instructional duties.

- *Make false promises*: Dependability is the hallmark of being a professional. Make sure that your are perceived as someone who is reliable. Always do what you say and don't make commitments that you will have trouble fulfilling.

Susanne Dana

Being Present at Meetings

Monthly faculty meetings are a routine part of the school year. Attendance is mandatory at these large-group sessions. When administrators make important announcements, discuss critical issues facing the school, and even share their vision for the future. Unfortunately, too many faculty members view these type of meetings as a waste of their time; they attend with a sullen attitude and often behave in inappropriate ways that they would never tolerate in their own classrooms.

Attending various meetings is an important obligation and is part of your professional responsibilities as a classroom teacher. You will participate at general faculty meetings, department or grade-level meeting, in-service activities, and guidance conferences. It is important that you behave as a skilled, conscientious educator. Sit up straight, lean forward, pay attention, and take notes. You should be the kind of engaged participant that you expect to see from students in your own classroom.

DO:

> *"The palest ink is better than the best memory."*
> Chinese Proverb

- **Be on time**: You should arrive at meetings a few minutes early. Being prompt demonstrates respect to your administrators and fellow colleagues.
- **Sit near the front**: Too many teachers prefer to sit in the back of the room during meetings in an effort to preserve their anonymity. These individuals rarely participate or contribute while good teachers chose to sit in a prominent location near the front with other successful and enthusiastic teachers.
- **Take notes**: Your school and team leaders will always share vital information that you will need later. It is important to take good, detail notes rather than trusting your memory. An ancient Chinese proverb states that "the palest ink is better than the best memory." Consider devoting a specific notebook or binder exclusively to school meetings and administrative matters rather than relying on easily misplaced or lost scraps of paper. When you actually need to access the information again, you will know exactly where to find it.
- **Listen actively and pay attention**: Demonstrate that you are a good listener by periodically smiling or nodding. This provides positive feedback to the speaker and will help you focus on the topic being discussed.

DON'T:

- ***Correct papers***: This is one of the most common mistakes that teachers make when attending meetings and it is rude and shows disrespect. In fact, grading papers is one of the worst things you can do at any school meeting. Teachers who do personal work at a meeting communicate that they are bored and do not value what the speaker has to say.

- ***Hold private conversations***: All teachers know how frustrating it is when a student is talking inappropriately during class. It is insolent, impolite, and unacceptable. Good teachers do not have private conversations with others during meetings.

- ***Ask questions that have little relevance to the group as a whole***: It is important to respect your colleagues and to value their time. Therefore you should restrict your questions at meetings to relevant issues. If you have an individual need or concern, write down your question instead and privately speak with your principal or administrator at a more appropriate time.

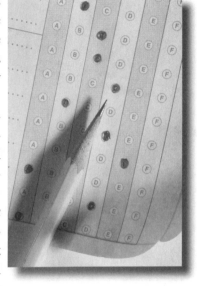

(Comstock Images)

- ***Text or read messages on your phone***: Concentrating on what is being discussed when you are texting, checking the weather, or doing other things on your phone is impossible. This is forbidden in your classroom and is unacceptable at meetings as well.

Susan Catlett

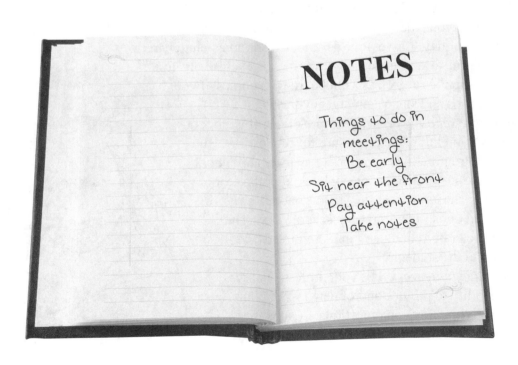

Absent? Be Prepared!

There are times when every teacher has to miss school. You may have a professional meeting, a family emergency, a doctor's appointment, or you may be sick. Remember that your classroom should be a safe, orderly and respectful place even when you are not there. With a little advanced planning, there are ways to make things go as smoothly as possible at school and maintain instruction during your absence.

DO:

- **_Prepare a detailed sub folder_**: At the beginning of the school year, collect all relevant materials in preparation for a substitute. Include the bell schedule, a school map, a list of key contact people, and class rolls and place. Place these materials in a distinctive folder clearly labeled "substitute plans." It is also helpful to prepare a list of reliable, responsible students who can run errands, if needed. Include discipline referral forms as well as school procedures for fire drill, lockdowns, or evacuations. Keep this folder in a prominent location in your classroom and provide a copy to your appropriate school administator.

- **_Always leave your classroom "substitute-ready"_**: It is important that you develop the habit of keeping your room in a neat and organized manner at the end of each school day. Leave your desk and work areas clutter free. It is helpful to designate one desk drawer exclusively for first aid supplies as well as a clipboard with copies of your student rolls and student emergency forms.

- **_Learn the school's procedures and rules_**: It is imperative that you know the procedure for requesting a substitute. Program the appropriate names and phone numbers into your cell phone or bookmark the school district's substitute website. Inquire about a list of preferred substitutes for your school. These individuals can be relied upon and are already well-known to the students.

- **_Leave adequate work_**: It is your professional responsibility to provide appropriate lesson plans and activities for your substitute. A substitute should never have to improvise or create busy work for the students. It is up to you to create meaningful assignments that can be implemented in your absence using materials and resources within your classroom.

- ***Show your appreciation for good behavior***: In your plans. request that the substitute leave a detailed report about the day. When students have behaved well during your absence, it is important to let them know that you appreciate their good behavior. A small token of thanks such as a piece of candy or a "participation grade" can serve as a welcomed reward to acknowledge positive students conduct.

DON'T:

- ***Wait until the last minute before calling in sick***: There is nothing heroic about being sick and going to work. You risk infecting your students and colleagues and you will not be effective if you are feeling ill. Teachers are provided sick days for this reason and these should be used appropriately. Administrators will appreciate any advanced notice you can provide regarding an impending absence since it will give them adequate time to find a good substitute.

- ***Expect to have a substitute with knowledge of your subject***: Substitutes are generally not required to have a teaching license and are not assigned according to their academic background. It is important that teachers leave detailed and specific lesson plans that can be followed by anyone. If you are having students work on material that will be assessed, an appropriate answer key should be provided so that the substitute teacher can assist students with a potential problems.

- ***Ignore discipline problems***: If your substitute leaves a referral about a particular student, it is your obligation to follow up on the report with the student, the parents and the administration. Any disrespect or insubordination towards a substitute is unacceptable and must be handled promptly and appropriately.

Susanne Dana

(Comstock Images)

Maintaining a Professional Outlook

In every occupation, there are those who choose to act as professionals regardless of the circumstances that they encounter. Professionalism means that you hold yourself to a high standard of ethical conduct while working cooperatively with colleagues and co-workers in fulfilling your contractual obligations. It is these important qualities and areas of conduct which separate the true professional teachers from those who are indifferent.

In truth, teaching is altruistic, far removed from the business world. It is a noble, service-oriented profession where you work to better the lives of our students. Despite such an admirable goal, there are still a handful of teachers whose efforts are lackluster and not focused on their students. They are frequently egocentric and have a selfish attitude. Instead of working for the common good of the students, these unprofessional educators slowly whittle and erode away at the core beliefs of the school community.

(Comstock Images)

Misguided "educators" undermine the efforts of hardworking teachers who work tirelessly with students to help them achieve. They create a dark undercurrent that ebbs and flows throughout their buildings and can even infest the school district. As a whole, these infamous teachers are the ones that your mentors once warned you about when they told you to steer clear of that hotbed of negativity, the teacher's lounge. Too often, though, these thoughtless teachers leave the general public with a skewed view of what is actually happening in our nation's classrooms. As a dedicated professional, it is your obligation to counteract such negativity and prevent it from corrupting your idealistic passion or harming your students' learning.

DO:

- *Stay positive*: You will face challenges in your day-to-day professional work. However, it is ultimately your personal outlook that will determine your responses to these challenges. Philip Bigler, the 1998 National Teacher of the Year, wrote about a critical piece of advice he once received from his principal at McLean High School, Elizabeth Lodal, in his book, *Teaching History in an Uncivilized World*. Lodal told him after a particularly trying period that, "To be a good teacher you have to be an optimist; you have to have faith in your students and believe that things will eventually work out for the best." This sage advice forever changed his outlook and approach to teaching.

- *Be optimistic*: Being optimistic does not mean that you have to agree with everything that occurs in your building or district. Nor does it mean that you are oblivious to reality or unaware of difficult challenges. Being optimistic means that even when you are faced with obstacles and challenges, you will not become discouraged by them. Those who are optimistic make decisions that create positive outcomes by focusing on what can be done rather than being frustrated by what they cannot control. Great teachers strive to make the best of every situation.

- *Be proactive rather than reactive*: In today's modern schools, you will have to contend with many demands that are superfluous to instruction. From federal and state mandates to district-wide initiatives, you must contend with an ever changing educational environment. As a professional educator, you must remain optimistic regardless of circumstances. Constant complaining does not change anything nor does it solve any problems. Instead, you need to use your judgment and take a more proactive approach. As a skilled teacher, you know that you can control only that which is within your power. Therefore, it is up to you to do your best to provide an excellent education for each and every student regardless of any external mandates.

DON'T:

- *Use the wrong voice*: When you have true professional concerns, it is important to address them in an appropriate manner. You need to follow proper channels when addressing issues and voicing concerns. Remember to remain polite and respectful. Whining, complaining, and blaming is confrontational and unprincipled. Instead, you should focus on what is best for your students and for the school; your arguments should always be supported by evidence, data, and reason.

Stephanie Doyle

> *Quality teaching begins with your overall outlook and attitude. Make the choice to be an optimist. This positive approach to teaching will influence everyone around you and will create an exciting and vibrant educational climate in your classroom.*

Holidays, Celebrations, and Commemorations

There are many important holidays that occur during the school year. These occasions provide valuable teaching and learning opportunities.

Labor Day, 1st Monday in September
Constitution Day, September 17
Columbus Day, 2nd Monday in October
Veteran's Day, November 11
Thanksgiving Day, 4th Thursday in November
Pearl Harbor Remembrance Day, December 7
Martin Luther King Day, 3rd Monday in January
Ground Hog Day, February 2
Lincoln's Birthday, February 12
Valentine's Day, February 14
President's Day, 3rd Monday in February
George Washington's Birthday, February 22
Dr. Seuss's Birthday, March 2
Thomas Jefferson's Birthday, April 13
Arbor Day, April (date varies)
Memorial Day, Last Monday in May
D-Day Remembrance Day, June 6
Flag Day, June 14

Month Long Commemorations

September: Hispanic Heritage Month
February: Black History Month
March: National Women's History Month
April: School Library Month
May: National Physical Fitness and Sports Month

It is also important to remember and respect the fact that many students will be observing religious holidays and traditions throughout the year. Never schedule tests, major assignments, or homework during these solemn occasions.

Chapter VI

Professional Library
"Must Haves"

Professional Reading List

I'd Like to Apologize to Every Teacher I Ever Had: My Year as a Rookie Teacher at Northeast High **(2012)** by Tony Danza, 262 pages. (Reviewed by Philip Bigler)

Tony Danza is perhaps best remembered for his roles in the ancient television sit-coms "Taxi" and "Who's the Boss?" But with his Hollywood acting career in decline, the aging and exceedingly likeable Danza rekindled his life-long desire to become a high school teacher. In 2009, he was hired at Philadelphia's Northeast High School ostensibly to teach English but of course, the entire escapade had to be filmed for a new A&E reality show entitled "Teach: Tony Danza." In many ways the book, *I'd Like to Apologize to Every Teacher I Ever Had,* is a suitable companion piece for the television program. It chronicles Danza's compelling and often painful experiences as a novice educator as well as elaborates on many of the story lines from the TV program.

There is no question that Tony Danza's heart is in the right place; he cares for his students and he desperately wants them to succeed. That is, however, not enough as his skeptical principal, Linda Carroll, accurately observed: "Until kids learn something, you don't deserve the title of teacher."

Actor Tony Danza spent one year teaching English in Philadelphia. His efforts were chronicled in a television series on A&E. (Carrienelson1 | Dreamstime.com)

As with so many other made-for-television endeavors, the entire premise is a fraud. Danza is assigned a single section of tenth grade English class with just 26 students. He is thus spared the normal routine, responsibilities, and realities of a typical full-time teacher. Danza is fortunate to have a veteran educator observing his class every day, and this mentor provides immediate feedback, constant guidance, and sage advice.

Many of Tony Danza's problems as a new "teacher" stem from his inadequate teacher preparation. He spends just a few weeks over the summer attending an intensive preparatory program and this proves wholly inadequate. His lesson plans, although well-meaning, are uninspired and which lack substance, creativity, content, and rigor. By reading Danza's book or viewing the various episodes of the television series, one would have to conclude that he spent an entire school year endlessly talking about himself while his course curriculum consisted of instruction only on *To Kill a Mockingbird* and *Julius Caesar*. This lack of meaningful content only exacerbates Danza's unending struggle with basic classroom management. For veteran educators, this soon becomes a painful and excruciating journey.

There are, however, many lessons that young teachers can derive from *I'd Like to Apologize to Every Teacher I Ever Had*. Probably the most significant is that merely possessing a strong desire to be a good and successful teacher will not replace hard work, dedication, persistence, and adequate preparation. Teaching is not a casual hobby, but a serious business which requires commitment and professionalism.

A&E cancelled "Teach: Tony Danza" after just seven episodes. Apparently, there was not enough excitement or manufactured drama in the classroom to justify continuing the program beyond the first semester. Sans the TV cameras, Danza honorably completes his commitment to Northeast but decides not to return for a second school year. So, once again, a group of promising, urban students are betrayed by well-intentioned adults and abandoned to face their fate alone. That, too, is an all together predictable story.

Danza, Tony (2012). *I'd Like to Apologize to Every Teacher I Ever Had*. New York: Crown Archetype &*Teach: Tony Danza* (2010), DVD, New York: A&E Television Networks, LLC.

Teach Like a Champion: 49 Techniques that Put Students on the Path to College (2010) by Doug Lemov, 323 pages. (Reviewed by Susan Catlett)

In his introduction to this "how-to" manual for effective teaching, Doug Lemov declares that "[m]any of the techniques [described in his] book at first may seem mundane, unremarkable, even disappointing. They are not always especially innovative"(5). His modest assessment, however, is deceiving. *Teach Like a Champion* contains descriptions and justifications of classroom tools that are relevant and accessible to all teachers—from a first year educator looking for practical ways to increase expectations to the most experienced teacher attempting to refine a well-practiced craft.

Doug Lemov is a former English and history teacher. He was one of the founders of the Academy of the Pacific Rim Charter School in Boston. He is currently the managing editor of Uncommon Schools, a non-profit organization that helps start and manage urban charter public schools. Lemov actively trains school leaders and teachers and works with schools throughout the United States.

Throughout his distinguished career as a classroom teacher, administrator, and consultant, Lemov has observed highly effective teachers in countless classrooms working primarily in high need, high poverty public schools. Drawing from this experience, he focuses Part I of *Teach Like a Champion* on identifying "specific, concrete, actionable" techniques that support success for all students (3). In Part II, Lemov suggests that all teachers must become effective reading teachers and he describes practical techniques that can increase every student's reading proficiency.

Lemov is very careful to make a distinction between strategies and techniques. Strategies are general approaches to solving problems while techniques are "[those] things you say or do in a particular way" (3). His 49 techniques are essentially practical tools that can be quickly and easily implemented in virtually any American classroom. The following are several examples of Lemov's realistic, sensible techniques.

• "Square Up/Stand Still" encourages teachers to stop moving, face students, and cease from engaging in other tasks when verbally giving to directions. This simple act removes distractions and communicates the importance of the instruction (186).

• "Everybody Writes" gives students a brief opportunity to reflect in writing before engaging in discussion. Before sharing with the class, students are able to articulate and organize their thoughts (137).

• "Cold Call" raises expectations when teachers call on students regardless of whether they have raised their hands. This questioning technique ensures that all students are engaged and prepared to answer any question while giving the teacher valuable feedback about their understanding (111).

(Comstock Images)

Teach Like a Champion includes a useful DVD entitled "See It In Action" with clips of "champion teachers" applying Lemov's numerous techniques. Viewing the clips is not necessary to understand or implement his methods, but the DVD does provide a concrete view of how they can be seamlessly integrated to elicit quality performance from all students.

Perhaps the most impressive feature of *Teach Like a Champion* is its versatility. A teacher can flip to one technique, find out how to apply it, consider its benefits, and focus on its key principles in just minutes. Conversely, a careful and thorough reading of the book will help build a teacher's arsenal of tools and change a teacher's entire operating procedure. Indeed, Lemov's techniques tend to work "in synergy[;] using one makes another better, and the whole is greater than the sum of the parts" (5).

It is common knowledge today that teachers are the single most important school-based factor in student achievement. *Teach Like a Champion* provides teachers with much needed practical and useful techniques. When used deliberately and habitually, those techniques will significantly improve teacher efficacy, student learning, and classroom climate. This book is an indispensable resource that belongs on every teacher's bookshelf—annotated, highlighted, and dog-eared.

Lemov, Doug (2010). *Teach Like a Champion: 49 Techniques that Put Students on the Path to College*. San Francisco: John Wiley & Sons.

The Water is Wide (1972) by Pat Conroy, 294 pages. (Reviewed by Philip Bigler)

Pat Conroy is a national treasure. He, along with Tom Wolfe, is arguably one of America's greatest contemporary writers. *The Water is Wide* is one of Conroy's earliest works and as such, it lacks some of the sophistication and plot development characteristic of his later novels. Still, Conroy's facility with the English language is readily apparent and the book remains a joy to read. Moreover, it is an inspiring story that all teachers can learn from.

The Water is Wide is the tale of a young, novice teacher, "Conrack," who is assigned to teach in a small two-room schoolhouse on isolated "Yamacraw" Island. In the book, the tidal river separating the mythical island from mainland South Carolina represents both a physical as well as a metaphorical chasm. Yamacraw is inhabited by the decendants of freed slaves and the island children continued to speak in an ancient Gullah dialect. Ignored and abandoned by the central school administration, however, the students remained completely ignorant of life beyond their small provincial world. As Conroy writes, "Each time I broached a new subject, it revealed some astonishing gap in the kids' knowledge... They had never heard of Shakespeare or Aesop. They never heard of England or India…they had never been to a museum, never looked at a work of art, never read a piece of good literature…and never done a thousand things that children of a similar age took for granted" (40-41).

Undeterred, Conrack refuses to accept his students' ignorance and tries a number of creative and innovative techniques to inspire them to learn. This is the primary lesson that should be derived from *The Water is Wide*—all good teachers must be missionaries of learning and apostles of excellence. It is our primary responsibility and obligation to see that all children in our classrooms actually do learn. To do this, it is imperative that educators adapt, innovate, inspire, cajole, and motivate their students in creative ways in order to ensure that they do. Conrack proves remarkably successful in his own endeavors, and he finally teaches these precious children the many joys of learning.

Like most of Pat Conroy's books, *The Water is Wide* is a thinly veiled semi-autobiographical account that mirrors much of his own life experiences. After graduating from the Citadel, Conroy briefly taught English in Beaufort, South Carolina before accepting a teaching position on Daufuskie Island. There, he ran into considerable conflict with the school system's bureaucracy and eventually lost his job for insubordination and his unorthodox teaching methods. Likewise, in the novel, his protagonist ultimately suffers the same fate, and the book thus does not have a happy ending.

In 1974, *The Water is Wide* was made into a Hollywood film entitled *Conrack*. It stars a young Jon Voight and remains a wonderful, inspirational film for all teachers. Unfortunately, it is available only on archaic videotape but it can sometimes be viewed on streaming video sites. Likewise, several scenes from the movie can be watched on YouTube. The film was remade for television in 2006, but this later effort is a poor imitation of the earlier film.

Conroy, Pat (2006). *The Water is Wide*. New York: The Dial Press.

Be a Teacher: You Can Make a Difference (2007) edited by Philip Bigler and Stephanie Bishop. 256 pages. (Reviewed by Jami Dodenhoff)

I have two copies of *Be A Teacher: You Can Make a Difference*. One is a well-read paperback that belongs at home, to be read over and over, while the other is tucked safely away in my second grade classroom, readily available for those discouraging afternoons when passion and purpose can be difficult to find. *Be A Teacher* continues to provide much needed assurance, inspiration, and encouragement that will uplift teachers even on the most exhausting of school days.

Be A Teacher is a compilation of stories written by an elite group of distinguished educators, including teachers, administrators, and principals from across all grade levels. One segment, "A Call to Teach: Excellence for a Lifetime," is even from a former Virginia State Superintendent of Public Instruction, Jo Lynne DeMary. All of the contributing educators in this book have been recognized for their excellence in the classroom. These include Milken Educators, Virginia Lottery Super Teachers, and Regional, State Teachers of the Year as well as a National Teacher of the Year. Collectively they are an impressive group, truly among America's best. Each teacher has written a personal chapter which details their experiences, successes, and struggles in the classroom.

The authors reflect throughout on their many years in education and offer new and valuable insight, guidance, and support. Their wise advice is inspiring to novice educators, and their stories are touching, enlightening, and frequently humorous. They show that even the most skilled teachers had to often endure a rocky and uneasy start before they discovered their own unique identities. Young teachers will find solace in this fact as they work to overcome the routine set-backs that they will experience in their own classrooms. Behavior management, low academic achievement, and a lack of family support are just a few of the topics discussed in *Be A Teacher*. Most importantly, though, these educators reveal the fundamental lessons they have learned over the years that have enabled them to make a positive difference in the lives of their students.

Be A Teacher also contains several useful appendices that serve as a quick resource and reference for teachers. Appendix A, for instance, contains several top ten lists of advice on such diverse topics as parent-teacher communications to working with challenging students. Additional appendices consist of inspiring quotes, recommended "teacher" movies, and lists of valuable resources.

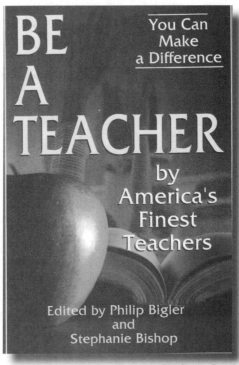

(Vandamere Press)

Every teacher will enjoy and cherish the stories that are honestly shared in *Be A Teacher*. They reveal that a passionate, dedicated educator can inspire students, enliven schools, and improve the quality of education. *Be A Teacher* reminds us that teaching is the greatest and most important profession there is and that determined educators can find the strength within themselves to change lives. This book deserves a prominent place in everyone's professional library.

Bigler, Philip & Stephanie Bishop Eds. (1997). *Be a Teacher: You Can Make a Difference*. St. Petersburg, FL: Vandamere Press.

Brain Rules: 12 Principles for Surviving and Thriving at Work, Home, and School **(2008)** by John Medina, 301 pages. (Reviewed by Susanne Dana)

One would assume that a book written by a developmental molecular biologist would hardly be accessible or even necessary for most new teachers, but Dr. John Medina's *Brain Rules* defies this conventional logic. The human brain is an extremely complex organ and has numerous functions that are identifiable and crucial for success in our modern world as well as in our nation's classrooms. Medina explains the current scientific research on how the brain operates and its most important functions. Likewise, he discusses how our evolutionary history and a myriad of stress factors inherent in modern society affect these functions. Each chapter concludes with suggestions about how brains work most effectively as well as critical information for teachers about dealing with their students.

Of course, most people already have some vague ideas about the interrelationships among the brain, body, and the natural environment. For example, exercise definitely seems to help individuals perform better, while multitasking often results in a loss of efficiency. But Dr. Medina explains this contradictory idea by describing the scientific discoveries about the operation of the brain as well as its predictable reaction to various stimuli and situations. Teachers will definitely not be bored or overwhelmed when reading *Brain Rules*. Indeed, Medina's chapter on "attention" has as its central thesis the concept that "people don't pay attention to boring things"(page 94). He is keenly aware of this fact and uses interesting vignettes interspersed with humor to keep the book lively and the reader engaged.

Dr. Medina astutely points out how the "traditional American classroom" is neither optimized nor organized with reference to current scientific thought. He offers practical advice on how schools and classrooms should be restructured to improve and maximize student learning. At times, some of his advice can become a bit irritating especially when variants of his ideas have already been implemented as a routine part of best teaching practices. The concept that "students learn better from words and pictures than from words alone" is hardly new or revolutionary; it is common knowledge for virtually all educators (page 210).

Some of Dr. Medina's other thoughts and ideas would require an enormous societal transformation. Schools, parents, and community would have to make a fundamental commitment to change. This may be impractical. He proposes, for instance, that "First grade would begin a week after birth" and that after students enroll in school, their "parents would take an occasional series of marital refresher courses" in order to prevent the harmful effects that stress can have on learning (page 192).

There is a tremendous amount of useful advice for teachers in *Brain Rules*. Conscientious educators will be able to incorporate many of these ideas and methods when planning creative activities that will enhance instruction and maximize student learning. The book is a helpful and useful tool for educators and will ultimately help them more fully understand how students learn and why they behave as they do.

Medina, John (2008). *Brain Rules: 12 Principles for Surviving and Thriving at Work, Home, and School*. Seattle, WA: Pear Press.

Brain Rules Chapters

- Exercise
- Survival
- Wiring
- Attention
- Short-term memory
- Long-term memory
- Sleep
- Stress
- Sensory Integration
- Vision
- Gender
- Exploration

***Why Don't Students Like School?* (2009)** by Daniel T. Willingham, 240 pages. (Reviewed by Tabitha Strickler)

Daniel Willingham's *Why Don't Students Like School?* has the evocative subtitle: *A Cognitive Scientist Answers Questions About How the Mind Works and What It Means for the Classroom.* It is no wonder that this text seems like a book of answers specially designed to help K-12 teachers. The book is recommended for student teachers and novice educators, as well as for veteran teachers who will find it useful to refresh and revitalize their teaching.

The book is organized into nine chapters based upon nine questions formulated by Willingham's research on the brain and learning. These are:

1. Why don't students like school?
2. How can I teach students the skills they need when standardized tests require only facts?
3. Why do students remember everything that's on television and forget everything I say?
4. Why is it so hard for students to understand abstract ideas?
5. Is drilling worth it?
6. What's the secret to getting students to think like real scientists, mathematicians, and historians?
7. How should I adjust my teaching for different types of learners?
8. How can I help slow learners?
9. What about my mind?

Teachers will particularly appreciate the inclusion of a section entitled "Implications for the Classroom" within the context of each chapter. Even though Willingham does not have any relevant K-12 teaching experience, his recommendations are still valid and useful for educators. Indeed, teachers are often frustrated by too much esoteric, academic theory without any practical suggestions for implementation in actual classroom situations. Willingham does not make this mistake and this is a welcome change.

(Corbis Images)

Why Don't Student's Like School? unfortunately reads much like a dreary college textbook. This can be tedious especially for an experienced teacher and it makes the book difficult to read and enjoy thoroughly. While the questions posed in each chapter are interesting, many of the principles and knowledge about students are already known nature to veteran teachers. For example, Willingham's premise in Chapter 1 is that the brain is wired for curiosity, but not necessarily thinking. He says that if work is always too difficult for a student, that the student will not find learning enjoyable. He proposes that teachers should look for tasks that lie just beyond where their students can perform. This idea of "stretching" a student's ability to complete tasks on his own is easily recognizable to the veteran teacher as working within Lev Vygotsky's "zone of proximal development."

Willingham uses each chapter as a springboard for the next. At times, the text feels repetitive, but Willingham demonstrates his knowledge about brain research to reiterate key points for the reader. He is also very thorough in examples throughout each chapter. By the end of each chapter, readers will understand the principles he illustrates.

Author Daniel Willingham has been a Professor of Psychology at the University of Virginia since 1992. His research on the brain, memory, and their relationship to learning makes his studies desirable for educators from kindergarten through college. Willingham has written many journal articles and has made presentations throughout the country. He also authored another book focused on education in 2012 called *When Can You Trust the Experts? How to Tell Good Science From Bad in Education.*

Note: Visit Daniel Willingham's website at http://www.danielwillingham.com. There, he provides contact information along with articles and videos based on his research.

Willingham, Daniel (2009). *Why Don't Students Like School: A Cognitive Scientist Answers Questions About How the Mind Works and What It Means for the Classroom.* Somerset, NJ: Jossey-Bass Publishers.

Tongue Fu! How to Deflect, Disarm, and Defuse any Verbal Conflict (1996) by Sam Horn, 236 pages. (Reviewed by Susanne Dana)

One school principal told his teachers during new teacher orientation, "Don't worry about content. Content is easy. Kids are hard." It was a startling comment, but his assertion is definitely supported by Sam Horn in her fascinating series of *Tongue Fu* books. Horn is a successful communication consultant and public speaker. Her 1996 book, T*ongue Fu! How to Deflect, Disarm, and Defuse any Verbal Conflict*, will help teachers discover what to say as well as what not to say when working with difficult students and colleagues. Just as the martial arts are a way to neutralize a physical attack, Ms. Horn explains how to develop tools and resources to defuse verbal altercations.

Tongue Fu is not a book of trite one-liners but rather an important discussion about how to achieve desired outcomes while treating people with kindness and dignity. When dealing with someone who is very frustrated, for example, Ms. Horn recommends that we first ask ourselves "Why are they being difficult?" and "How would I feel under similar circumstances?" These are important questions to contemplate before any reaction or response. In cases where someone is complaining, she further suggests that teachers follow the so-called four A's: agree, apologize, act, and appreciate. This should be done without explanation, admitting fault, or assigning blame. Horn clearly and convincingly explains how her methods generally will result in a beneficial outcome by defusing a potentially uncomfortable situation.

Digital Juice

In today's schools, there are students who exhibit manipulative behavior or are considered bullies. Ms. Horn has developed techniques to use for these type of individuals. For manipulative individuals, Horn uses "Name the game," a technique where you calmly and clearly focus attention on what they are doing. With bullies, it is imperative to hold the offenders accountable for their actions and firmly say "Enough!"

Much of *Tongue Fu* on the surface seems to be common sense, but most people react to difficult situations emotionally rather than rationally. By following Sam Horn's advice, readers will gain a greater awareness of their actions and reactions, which will help them deal effectively with everyday crises. Horn points out numerous ways to control our emotions, gain confidence, and reduce stress levels, to be happier and more productive people. Although most of her examples center on sales and marketing situations and corporate employer/employee dilemmas, her methods are appropriate to a teacher's life.

There are several other related books authored by Ms. Horn that are geared towards specific needs and concerns. These include *Tongue Fu! At School: 30 Ways to Get Along with Teachers, Principals, Students, and Parents*; *Take the Bully by the Horns: Stop Unethical, Uncooperative; or Unpleasant People from Running and Ruining Your Life*; and *Tongue Fu! Get Along Better with Anyone, Anywhere, Anytime.*

Horn, Sam (1996) *Tongue Fu! How to Deflect, Disarm, and Defuse any Verbal Conflict.* New York: St. Martin's Griffin.

Teaching History in an Uncivilized World **(2012)** by Philip Bigler, 386 pages. (Reviewed by Jami Dodenhoff)

Philip Bigler is one of the nation's elite educators whose 35-year career has been devoted to inspiring and educating students. In 1998, Mr. Bigler was selected as National Teacher of the Year during a Rose Garden Ceremony at the White House. President Bill Clinton declared, "We need more teachers like Philip Bigler and all our other honorees in every classroom in America today, for it is they who can make our schools the best in the world."

Teaching History in an Uncivilized World is Bigler's compelling memoir of his career. Beginning with the lessons he learned as a novice teacher at Oakton High School in Fairfax County (VA), the book is filled with insights and advice that will help other educators become better teachers. He explains how he became successful as a high school social studies teacher. His challenging journey included two RIF's (layoffs) and a three year hiatus from the classroom when he became the historian at Arlington National Cemetery. Bigler's memoir is relevant not only to history teachers, but also to all teachers. Indeed, much of his advice is applicable to all grade levels and subject areas.

(Apple Ridge Publishers)

Teaching History serves as an honest and critical account of how social studies instruction and serious academics are in jeopardy as course content becomes diluted by political agendas and educational fads. Bigler provides a myriad of examples from his own career where students fail to comprehend the important lessons of history and fail to grasp the critical problems of their contemporary world. This serves to remind teachers of the critical role that they play in American society and that ignorance remains the greatest threat to a civil society. Bigler asserts that "…Those of us who have studied history know well, human progress is neither inevitable nor preordained. A nation's culture and its fundamental principles are fragile things which must be nurtured and preserved" (9). Teachers who read this important book will be renewed in their passion and purpose for their respective subjects.

In addition, Bigler eloquently articulates his fundamental beliefs about education. His words are inspiring and uplifting. The vast majority of teachers, Bigler claims, are talented and dedicated professionals who are dedicated to making a positive difference in the lives of children. This is something worthy of both respect and praise. All educators will readily identify with many of Philip Bigler's professional and classroom experiences and will be able to incorporate his principles and philosophies into their own practice. Indeed, there are many pearls of wisdom embedded in his stories. Some of these are encouraging while others are disheartening, but each example enabled Bigler to grow and evolve as an educator.

Philip Bigler's life story is one of metamorphosis. He began his career as an adequate, well-meaning novice. Through his dedication and hard work, he was transformed into an elite educator who was able to successfully bring history to life in his classroom. As President Clinton noted during his remarks at Bigler's Rose Garden ceremony: "For more than 20 years, [Philip Bigler's] students haven't just studied history, they have lived it. He's transformed his classroom into a virtual time machine, challenging students to debate each other as members of rival ancient Greek city states; as lawyers before the Supreme Court; as presidential candidates named Thomas Jefferson and John Adams. Through these historical simulations, his students have learned lessons about democracy and the meaning of citizenship, lessons that will last a lifetime --lessons we want every American to know." *Teaching History* effectively proves that great educators in our schools are the single most critical factor in the success of students. Everyone who reads this memoir will be inspired to become more purpose-driven in their teaching practice.

Bigler, Philip (2012) *Teaching History in an Uncivilized World.* Quicksburg, VA: Apple Ridge Publishers. Also visit his website at http://www.philipbigler.com.

National Teacher of the Year, Philip Bigler, with President Bill Clinton, Secretary of Education Richard Riley, and Virginia Senator Charles Robb at the White House Rose Garden Ceremony, April 24, 1998. (White House Photo)

Worksheets Don't Grow Dendrites: 20 Instructional Strategies That Engage the Brain (2010)
by Marcia L. Tate. 158 pages. (Reviewed by Jami Dodenhoff)

Marcia Tate is well known in the field of education for her pioneering work on brain-based learning. She regularly conducts workshops, instructs courses, and has written several best-selling books. Recently, she published the second edition to her highly successful book, *Worksheets Don't Grow Dendrites*, which should be a staple in every teacher's library (dendrites are specialized cell parts that bring electrical signals to the neurons in the brain; when somebody learns something new, they grow a dendrite).

(SOMC)

Dendrites serves as a powerful reference guide for all grade level teachers and subject areas. In 20 succinct chapters, Dr. Tate explains specific brain-based instructional strategies which can be implemented in any classroom. The book is well organized, practical, and readable. It enables teachers to quickly locate useful material and ideas which can be used in their lesson planning. This is particularly useful for time-stressed educators. As an added bonus, Marcia Tate's writing is positive, humorous, and personal. Educators will definitely enjoy reading about her relevant experiences as a mother, a speaker, and an instructor.

Each chapter begins with a concise introduction that explains the purpose of a given strategy. Dr. Tate remains a teacher at heart and provides clear examples and references to support each of her assertions. She includes several quotations from dependable sources and education experts who provide important theoretical support and credibility for the strategies. Likewise, there are several brief illustrations on how teachers can implement the instructional strategies in their own classroom. Dr. Tate's examples include various subject areas and grade levels so that educators can choose the ideas that best meet the needs of their own students. These, of course, need further development in order to be properly incorporated into actual lesson plans, but teachers will be inspired to individualize the activities for their own classroom.

There is space provided at the end of each chapter where teachers can plan to integrate Dr. Tate's strategies into their teaching practice. Teachers can list their objectives and align them to a specific activity. Diligent educators will utilize her ideas and techniques so that their lesson plans will yield massive amounts of dendrite-growth throughout the year!

Tate, Marcia (2010). *Worksheets Don't Grow Dendrites: 20 Instructional Strategies That Engage the Brain* (2nd ed.). Thousand Oaks, California: Corwin. Visit Marcia Tate's website at http://www.developingmindsinc.com/ to learn more about her workshops, classes, and books.

The Active Classroom: Practical Strategies for Involving Students in the Learning Process (2009) by Ron Nash, 154 pages. (Reviewed by Kathy Galford)

Ron Nash was a secondary social studies teacher and instructional coordinator for Virginia Beach Public Schools before becoming a national trainer on brain compatible learning. This book is the first of his "Active" series and offers practical strategies for changing the focus of a classroom from teacher-centered to student-centered. Based on current brain-based learning research, Nash discusses the "how's" and "why's" of engaging students in active learning. Drawing on his own experience of transforming himself from instructor to facilitator, Nash outlines methods for creating an active classroom by incorporating structured conversation, movement, music, visual cues, technology, and storytelling into the learning process. He also offers advice on planning and presenting with confidence.

The Active Classroom is an easy-to-read book and is applicable to novice and veteran teachers alike. With passion and expertise, Nash explains how a developing brain is not wired to "sit and get" in a quiet environment for long periods of time. Instead, students should be up and moving, pairing and sharing, and interacting with peers in an energizing atmosphere. Nash provides concrete explanations, helpful advice, and exciting strategies that can be put into practice immediately. He incorporates step-by-step instructions, clear diagrams, sample lesson plans on a variety of subjects and levels, and a useful index that guides teachers through the process of creating an exciting learning setting in which all learners become enthusiastically involved. In his appendix, Nash gives an inside view of an active classroom. He discusses what one should and should not observe in this environment. He also shares his contact information and welcomes readers to contact him if they have questions or need advice.

Armed with a new arsenal of classroom ideas and feeling like they have gained a new friend and mentor in Ron Nash, educators will be energized and motivated to incorporate these exciting instructional approaches in their classrooms. This captivating book is a must-have for today's teachers who wish to inspire and engage learners as well as sustain passion for their profession.

Nash, Ron (2009). *The Active Classroom: Practical Strategies for Involving Students in the Learning Process.* Thousand Oaks, CA: Corwin Publishers. Other books in Ron Nash's "Active" series include *The Active Teacher* (2009), *The Active Classroom Fieldbook* (2010), *From Seatwork to Featwork* (2012), *The Active Mentor* (2010), and *The Active Workshop* (2010).

Teaching with Love and Logic: Taking Control of the Classroom (1995, revised 2010) by Jim Fay and David Funk, 399 pages (Reviewed by Suzi Sherman)

Teaching with Love and Logic was co-authored by Jim Fay and David Funk based on years of research, practical experience and observations. It offers clear, concise, and effective tools to foster positive discipline in your classroom and school. The authors provide useful summaries of the research that led to the development of this program; questions to pose when starting and implementing it; and practical examples of how it is to be used effectively.

(Comstock Images)

Love and Logic is not intended to be a stand-alone discipline program. Rather, it complements many other discipline programs, offering teachers an opportunity to build positive student relationships while reducing teacher stress. According to Fay and Funk, there are three main rules that govern this philosophy: "1. People learn from their own decisions; 2. Use enforceable limits providing choices within the limits; and 3. Apply consequences with empathy" (25). As teachers, it is important to provide practical and logical consequences to help correct behavioral concerns. Doing so will make the students more likely to accept personal responsibility for their own actions and thus learn to make wiser choices in the future.

The book is organized into five distinct parts. Each section provides the reader with a clear understanding of the logic behind the philosophy as well as offering an abundance of examples. To further support the authors' contentions, phrases, and questions are provided, which can be used when dealing with a wide array of disciplinary concerns. There is also a useful chapter on legal issues that is especially important for all teachers, given our litigious society. Fay and Funk address the many diverse styles of teaching and show how each style can be implemented into their model. Finally, *Teaching with Love and Logic* gives an in-depth look into a model school where their techniques have been successfully implemented.

Teaching with Love and Logic is a book that all teachers will want for their personal and professional libraries. It will be a useful and important reference, as it is easy to read with ample explanations. Moreover, the book is based upon solid research, and the method makes sense. It is so logical that you will be left wondering why you didn't think of these things before.

Fay, Jim and David Funk (2010). *Teaching with Love and Logic: Taking Control of the Classroom.* Golden, CO: Love and Logic Press. Jim Fay and David Funk have written other books based on the Love and Logic theme. They also have a website (www.loveandlogic.com) which provides a wealth of information, free articles and contact information for the Love and Logic Institute.

What Teachers Make: In Praise of the Greatest Job in the World (2012) by Taylor Mali, 224 pages. (Reviewed by Stephanie Doyle)

American bookstores have shelves lined with a variety of inspirational books, stories, and poems about teaching. Many of those books tug at one's heartstrings or make readers laugh at the daily anecdotes of what teachers experience each and every day. Despite this flood of literature, one book stands apart from the rest and represents a rallying cry for teachers everywhere: Taylor Mali's *What Teachers Make: In Praise of the Greatest Job in the World.* This short but powerful book is more than inspirational prose; it is a validation of the teaching profession and one that every educator should read. Mali's collection of poems and essays celebrates the teaching profession in a fresh and unique way.

Taylor Mali is a native New Yorker and taught for nine years at the middle school, high school and college levels. It was through his experiences in the classroom while teaching English, math, history, and SAT Preparation that he found much of the inspiration for *What Teachers Make: In Praise of the Greatest Job in the World*. Mali's beautiful and inspiring prose is infused with his experiences as a classroom teacher and he gives educators new hope while celebrating the nobility of the teaching profession which is often vilified and denigrated by critics and naysayers.

In his book, Mali writes about the challenges, struggles, triumphs, and treasured moments of teaching. By far, his most famous poem is "What Teachers Make." It represents one of the most powerful and eloquent defenses of the teaching profession and has stirred the hearts and minds of educators everywhere. This rousing poem has been distributed to millions of people thanks to a video version readily available on YouTube. Mali is a terrific writer and an advocate of teachers. He recognizes the critical role that teachers play in educating our nation's children. His creativity and deep emotional themes make this book exceptional. In short, Taylor Mali is an inspiration.

Mali, Taylor (2012). *What Teachers Make: In Praise of the Greatest Job in the World*. New York: Berkley Trade.

(Serif Images)

What Great Teachers Do Differently: 14 Things That Matter Most (2004) by Todd Whittaker, 144 pages. (Reviewed by Karen Drosinos)

In his book, *What Great Teachers Do Differently*, author Todd Whittaker approaches the subject of what "great" teachers do that sets them apart from their colleagues. He highlights 14 items that he considers the most important factors in differentiating a "great teacher" from just a "good teacher." Chapter topics include such things as: "It's People, Not Programs," and "Make It Cool to Care." These are some of the critical elements that Whittaker skillfully highlights to help teachers re-focus on truly effective teaching. The chapters are highly readable and easily navigated.

Todd Whittaker is currently a professor of educational leadership at Indiana University. Before moving to higher education, he was a middle and high school mathematics and business teacher with real world experience in the public schools. Whittaker believes that all teachers can become "great teachers" by simply "doing" things a bit differently. His book serves as a useful roadmap and is an outstanding resource for all teachers regardless of their experience, certification, or geographic location. *What Great Teachers Do Differently* will assist and aid teachers in making positive improvements and will help them to refine the way they look at their own teaching practices in the classroom.

Whittaker believes that although there is no single way to teach, there are certain manners in which all teachers can improve. Each chapter of his book is dedicated to things that matter most in classroom teaching practices. Although he states in his book that "education and classroom teaching is complex," there are areas that "great teachers" emulate, which give us insight into how to refine our skills and develop better strategies and ways to teach our students.

Whittaker, Todd (2004). *What Great Teachers Do Differently: 14 Things That Matter Most.* New York: Routledge, Press.

Fires in the Middle School Bathroom: Advice for Teachers from Middle Schoolers (2009) by Kathleen Cushman and Laura Rogers, 240 pages. (Reviewed by Stephanie Doyle)

Every adult knows that adolescence is a time of great emotional turbulence and personal as well as physical changes. Hormones begin to rage as "tweens" struggle to discover their true identities. Despite research and knowledge regarding the adolescent experience, how the children actually perceive the world remains a mystery to many parents and even to their teachers. The business of teaching in a middle school setting has been compared to the work of the world's great detectives, with teachers constantly seeking clues by which to uncover the profound mysteries necessary to educate this special age group of students. Authors Kathleen Cushman and Laura Rogers have uncovered the truth behind many of those adolescence mysteries, in their work, *Fires in the Middle School Bathroom: Advice for Teachers from Middle Schoolers*.

Fires in the Middle School Bathroom: Advice for Teachers from Middle Schoolers is, in fact, a sequel to *Fires in the Bathroom: Advice to Teachers of High School Students*. Through the generous support of the MetLife Foundation and the organization "What Kids Can Do," both books were created to give a voice to students on issues that matter to them personally. This book, unlike most, allows teachers to glimpse inside the complex minds of students in grades five to eight and to gain helpful insights about how to build stronger relationships with their students. Cushman and Rogers effectively reveal the previously obscure thoughts and motivations of adolescents and they speak to the heart about how to teach middle school students effectively. With the actual voices of middle school students, the authors help to unravel some of the complexities that have often bewildered and frustrated teachers.

Traveling to five urban areas in Connecticut, New York, Rhode Island, California, and Indiana, Cushman and Rogers solicited the thoughts and suggestions from forty middle school students. Through these honest and open conversations, they illuminate how students in grades five through eight feel about issues surrounding the classroom and home. This book offers practical advice that comes directly from adolescents who openly shared their feelings about school and about how they wish to be treated as learners, and as developing teenagers. These insights, along with research conducted by Laura Rogers, a developmental psychologist, combine to give middle school teachers a framework to understand this often contradictory group of students.

There are also many supplementary materials and resources provided for immediate, practical classroom use. The supplements and resources allow teachers the opportunity to understand adolescence as well as build stronger relationships with their students by getting to know them more deeply. These resources will help teachers relate to middle school students more effectively.

Cushman, Kathleen and Laura Rogers (2009). *Fires in the Middle School Bathroom: Advice for Teachers from Middle Schoolers*. New York: New Press.

The Bee Eater: Michelle Rhee Takes on the Nation's Worst School District (2011) by Richard Whitmire, 270 pages. (Reviewed by Philip Bigler)

In 1992, Michelle Rhee was a recent graduate from Cornell University and had accepted a Teach for America placement at Harlem Park Elementary School in Baltimore, Maryland. One day, her second grade math students became hysterical when a bee flew into the classroom through an open window. In the ensuing chaos, Rhee killed the bee and then ate the dead insect in front of her startled students. Obviously, this was a different breed of teacher, one deserving of their attention and maybe even their respect.

Richard Whitmire uses this strange episode as both metaphor and title for his book, *The Bee Eater*. In this highly readable and interesting book, Whitmire chronicles Michelle Rhee's career in education and public policy. He portrays her as a courageous, determined, and dedicated individual but also as a person who could be uncompromising, difficult, and even derisive.

After providing the necessary background, Whitmire explains how Rhee became the chancellor of the District of Columbia Public Schools without having ever been a principal or superintendent. She had, though, been a successful teacher during her brief tenure in Baltimore and had run the New York based "The New Teacher Project" whose cleaver motto was "Compton kids deserve a Beverly Hills education." Despite her short resume, Rhee quickly earned a reputation as an individual who did not tolerate failure regardless of economic and sociological circumstances. Moreover, she was convinced that a quality teaching force teaching meaningful content was the solution to many of the persistent problems of America's urban schools. This principled commitment led to D.C. Mayor, Adrian Fenty, to appoint Rhee to fix his city's inadequate schools.

(Yael Weiss | Dreamstime.com)

In truth, Fenty is the true hero of the *Bee Eater*. He refused to do the politically expedient thing by accepting the status quo when the system was obviously failing. One administor explained that in the District, "There was no quality. There was no curriculum. There was no true evaluation…no one [was] being held accountable…[there was] no good instruction" (67). Fenty was willing to risk everything, including his political career in a high stakes effort to transform the schools and Rhee would be the perfect instrument to shake things up. And that she did.

Rhee was relentless and refused to accept mediocrity or excuses for consistent failure. Principals were ordered to seize control of their schools immediately, and those who could not do so were unceremoniously dismissed. Poorly performing teachers were likewise fired while under-enrolled schools were closed. Rhee ignored public concerns, and she failed to appreciate the political consequences of her actions. The children were her sole priority, and this was admirable.

Whitmire relates one story about how Rhee went through the school system's administrative offices and questioned various officials about what they were doing to help students. Most responded by citing their grandiose titles but could not adequately define or defend their jobs. Rhee had little time or patience for such incompetence, and she cleaned house. Similarly, when she conducted a highly publicized tour of the school system's warehouses, she discovered pallets of new textbooks, boxes of supplies, and other instructional materials stockpiled because of bureaucratic ineptitude. She immediately dispensed with the red tape and ordered all of the supplies distributed to the teachers and their classrooms.

Yet despite Rhee's obvious courage, she alienated many by her seemingly insatiable appetite for personal publicity. She appeared on the December 8, 2008 cover of *Time* magazine with the headline, "How to Fix America's Schools." She was ominously posed, unsmiling, in an empty classroom brandishing a broom. Likewise, Rhee was featured prominently in the evocative documentary *Waiting for Superman,* including a scene where she is filmed callously dismissing a veteran, albeit anonymous, principal.

The D.C. teacher union naturally loathed Michelle Rhee as did some of the members of the city council. When Mayor Fenty was forced to stand for re-election, he had to defend his chancellor and futily urged District residents to have patience so that her policies could have time to develop. Predictably, the voters rebelled, and Fenty lost the election to rival councilman and Rhee critic, Vincent Gray. Rhee resigned her position shortly thereafter.

Fenty returned to private life but could be content in the fact that he had forfeited his political career in an effort to do the right thing for the District's children. Conversely, Rhee was catapulted by her fame to the national stage and quickly established a new, high profile, non-profit organization, "Children First." She commands five figure speaking fees ($50,000 according to one source), travels first class, rides in limousines, and appears on *Oprah,* while the children in D.C. continue to struggle. Her three year experiment was over.

Recently, PBS aired as part of its *NOVA* series a program entitled, "The Education of Michelle Rhee." It challenged some of Michelle Rhee's most celebrated accomplishments and criticized her leadership style. Still, few could argue with her initial motives and personal courage. What Rhee's eventual legacy will be remains to be written, but the *Bee Eater* is a book all teachers will benefit from reading.

Whitmire, Richard (2011). *The Bee Eater: Michelle Rhee Takes on the Nation's Worst School District.* San Francisco, CA: Jossey-Bass. *Frontline: The Education of Michelle Rhee* first aired on PBS on January 1, 2013. It is available for viewing at the PBS website at: http://video.pbs.org/video/2323979463/.

Chapter VII

"Teacher Talk - A to Z

(Comstock Images)

Do You Speak Teacher?
Deciphering the Teacher Code

A Nation at Risk: Landmark educational study conducted during the Reagan administration which found that American schools were underperforming when compared to their global counterparts. The study lead to the standards movement with an emphasis on mathematics, science, English, social studies, and foreign languages.

Adequate Yearly Progress (AYP): Measurement of student progress mandated by the No Child Left Behind Act. Schools that under perform are subject to sanctions that could lead to major restructuring.

Advanced Placement (AP): AP classes are college-level coursework which students can take while in high school. Depending on the score on a final comprehensive examination, a student may receive college credits for successful completion of these rigorous high school courses. The AP program was established in 1955 and is currently managed by the College Board. There are 34 courses and exams offered through Advanced Placement curricula, but most schools offer a narrow range of courses. Individual course exams vary in format, but AP scoring always ranges from 1 (lowest) to 5 (highest). A score of 3 is considered to be passing but most universities require a 4 or 5 for credit.

(Digital Juice)

116

American College Testing (ACT): This standards-based college readiness exam is accepted by most colleges along with, or in place of, the SAT test for the admissions process. It measures math, English, reading, science, and writing skills with composite scores ranging from 11 to 36.

Americans with Disabilities Act Amendments Act (ADAAA): The amended form of the American with Disabilities Act (1990), the ADAAA became law in January 2009. The ADAAA broadened the scope of the original ADA providing protections for school-aged children with learning disabilities and Asperger's Syndrome as well as health issues such as diabetes, food allergies and asthma.

Annual Measurable Objectives (AMO): In compliance with the No Child Left Behind Act, each state must develop a measurement to determine if schools, districts or the state attains its proficiency goal of adequate yearly progress (AYP).

Armed Services Vocational Aptitude Battery (ASVAB): Introduced in 1968, this is a test that helps predict success in the military, both academically and occupationally. The subtests are designed to measure aptitudes in four areas: verbal, math, science and technical, and spatial. It is administered in both a paper and pencil version and computer version. In the paper and pencil administration of the test, there are nine subtests, each timed. The computer administration of the test (called the CAT-ASVAB) varies slightly. ASVAB scores determine qualification for enlistment and placement in an appropriate job in the military.

Attention Deficit Disorder (ADD): A disorder usually characterized by consistency of a short attention span which may cause interference in academic or social performance.

Attention Deficit Hyperactivity Disorder (ADHD): A disorder usually characterized by consistency in behaviors of hyperactivity, impulsivity, and sustaining attention which may cause difficulty in academic and/or social settings.

Autism Spectrum Disorder (ASD): Autism is a neurological disorder affecting both non-verbal and verbal communication, behavior and social interactions. Autism is a spectrum disorder where diagnosed students demonstrate a wide range of learning strengths and weaknesses in the areas of memory, cognition, behavior and social development.

Behavior Intervention Plan (BIP): A Behavior Intervention Plan is based on the data gathered from a Functional Behavior Assessment (FBA). The purpose of a BIP is to reduce inappropriate classroom behaviors by identifying the conditions surrounding the occurrence of these behaviors. A BIP is specifically tailored to each individual student's needs and interests.

Charter Schools: These public schools are schools of choice often focused on a certain theme or specialization. They have greater autonomy than traditional public schools but their charters must be renewed on a regular basis.

SOMC

Common Core State Standards: This initiative, developed by leaders from the National Governors Association and the Council of Chief State School Officers (CCSSO), was published in 2009 with the purpose of "provid[ing] a consistent, clear understanding of what students are expected to learn, so teachers and parents know what they need to do to help them." With a focus on English language arts and mathematics, the standards describe the knowledge and skills that students at each grade level must acquire to stay on track toward "college and career readiness." Forty-five states, the District of Columbia, four territories, and the Department of Defense Education Activity have adopted the Common Core State Standards. Minnesota rejected the Common Core Standards for mathematics, but accepted the English language arts standards. Texas and Alaska are not members of the initiative. Nebraska and Virginia are members but have decided not to adopt the standards.

Curriculum Map: This tool identifies central skills and content, instructional methods, and suggested assessments. The curriculum map helps teachers to develop both long-range and daily lessons plans. Some teachers differentiate between a curriculum map (a record of what has been taught) and a pacing guide (what will be taught in the future).

Developmentally Appropriate Practice (DAP): DAP refers to evidence-based teaching practice that is designed to meet individual children where they are developmentally. DAP enables teachers to prepare instruction that is unique to each child's readiness in order to promote his/her growth, learning and development. DAP is important to consider for each grade level, but also for each individual child because every child will develop at his/her own rate.

(SOMC)

The Elementary and Secondary Education Act (ESEA/NCLB): The Elementary and Secodary Education Act was first passed in 1965 as part of Lyndon Johnson's "War on Poverty." It authorized federally funded programs that are directed by the states. It emphasized equal access to education, focusing on improving academic achievement for the nation's most disadvantaged students. Like many federal funding programs, the ESEA is regularly updated and reauthorized. In 2002, Congress revised the act and renamed it the No Child Left Behind (NCLB); measures were added for testing, accountability, and school improvement, requiring schools to ensure all students are proficient in grade-level math and reading. NCLB also requires that all teachers be "highly qualified," fully certified or licensed by their state.

Emotional Disability (ED): A student may qualify for special education services and supports (IEP or 504 Plan) with the diagnosis of emotionally disability which is specified as a disability category under IDEA. Educational diagnosis may be carried out by a multidisciplinary school team with the student being given the categorical label of emotional disability. Students designated witn ah emotionally disability may exhibit difficulties in learning that are not related to intelligence, health or sensory deficits. Students may exhibit difficulties building relationships with peers and adults as well as demonstrate extreme mood swings and/or reactions to situations.

Family Educational Rights and Privacy Act (FERPA): Passed in 1974, this federal law provides privacy protection for educational records; it applies to all schools that receive funding for any U.S. Department of Education program. FERPA requires that a student's record not be shared with a third party without written consent. School officials, including teachers, may access student educational records if they have "legitimate educational interest" in the information. FERPA applies to all educational agencies and institutions that receive funding under any program administered by the Department. Classroom practices that may conflict with FERPA include public posting of grades, students calling out grades after self-correcting an assignment, and student aides grading papers that contain identifiable student information.

504 Plan: The 504 Plan is provided for by the Rehabilitation Act of 1973 and has a broader definition of student disabilities than the IEP provided for by the Individuals with Disability Act. In order to qualify for services and/or accommodations under the 504 plan, students must first receive educational or medical evaluation and meet the criteria for limitations in at least one area of speaking, listening, writing, or concentration. The accommodations outlined in the 504 Plan must be provided for the student in both the regular and special education environments. It is the responsibility of the regular educator to become familiar with all services and accommodations afforded students by IEP's or 504 Plans.

Functional Behavior Assessment (FBA): This is an assessment tool aimed at discovering the functions behind inappropriate class-room behaviors. Teachers observe the identified student and record the frequency, time, and other conditions when the behavior occurs. This data enables teachers to meet with the behavior assessment team, including parents, to determine how to effectively reduce such problem behaviors.

Gifted and Talented (GT): This term describes individuals who demonstrate the potential for outstanding aptitude in one or more areas of learning such as academic, artistic, athletic, and social. Although definitions and identification of GT students vary, most school systems offer differentiated educational programs to serve these students involving curriculum acceleration and enrichment.

Graduate Readiness Exam (GRE): A standardized assessment used to measure verbal reasoning, quantitative reasoning, and analytical writing which is used as an admissions requirement for many graduate programs in the United States. It is administered by Educational Testing Service (ETS).

Health Insurance and Portability Accountability Act (HIPAA): Signed into law in 1996, HIPPA is designed to protect the privacy of identifiable health information in any form—paper, electronic, recorded, or spoken. In most cases, the HIPAA privacy rule does not impact schools, but the law is applicable since schools do maintain and protect important student health information. For additional information, see: *http://www.hhs.gov/ocr/privacy/hipaa/faq/ferpa_and_hipaa/513.html.*

Individualized Education Program (IEP): Mandated under the provisions of the Individuals with Disabilities Act, an IEP team is designed to help children with learning disabilities or other special needs. Created in cooperation with parents, teachers, guidance counselors, and administrators, an IEP develops goals, accommodations, and objectives designed to help the student succeed in what is defined as the least restrictive environment. The IEP is a legal document provided for under the Individuals with Disabilities Act (IDEA) and includes supports, services, and accommodations that must be followed in both special and regular education environments.

International Baccalaureate (IB): Founded in 1968, the IB program consists of four programs aimed at children from 3-19 years old. The concept for the diploma program originated from Marie-Therese Maurette's book, *Is There a Way of Teaching for Peace?* Enrolled students are expected to develop the ability to analyze, synthesize, and evaluate knowledge in a common international curriculum. There are three sequences: the IB Primary Years Programme (ages 3-12), the IB Middle Years Programme (ages 11-16), and the IB Diploma Programme (ages 16-19). The most recent addition to the curricula is the IB Career-related Certificate for students ages 16-19.

Know, Want, How, Learned (KWHL): This is a graphic organizer that enables students to organize their thoughts and learning journey. Usually, written as a table with four columns, it stands for "What I *K*now, What I *W*ant to know, *H*ow I will learn it, and What I have *L*earned."

Learning Disability (LD): A learning disability is a lifelong, neuro-biological disorder that affects the manner in which individuals select, retain, and express information. It is an "umbrella term" used to describe an array of learning disorders.

National Standards: Several educational organizations have published national standards of education for subject areas, including the National Council of Teachers of English, the National Council of Teachers of Math, the National Council for the Social Studies, the National Academies of Science, and the International Society for Technology in Education. Although these national standards are accepted by organizations such as the National Board for Professional Teaching Standards, there is currently no standard national assessment for students. Under the United States Constitution in Article I, Section 8 and reaffirmed by the X Amendment, the power of education is reserved for the individual state governments.

No Child Left Behind Act (NCLB): Landmark piece of legislation passed in 2001 during the Bush administration; the law was actually a reauthorization of the 1965 Elementary & Secondary Education Act. NCLB emphasized improving basic skills, especially reading comprehension, coupled with regular assessment. The goal was to improve accountability while increasing student achievement.

Positive Behavior Support (PBS): This is an approach to school-wide discipline that is gaining popularity in U.S. schools. As of the fall 2011, over sixteen thousand schools had enacted PBS, and their numbers continue to grow. Through PBS, schools seek to establish a positive school culture where students are "caught being good" in and out of their classrooms. PBS is a three-tiered model for school-wide success. The bottom tier is "universal": classroom and non-classroom; the second or middle tier is "targeted" for at-risk student support; the top tier is "individual level" for focused and specialized student supports. A

(Comstock Images)

leadership team works with teachers to provide specialized interventions for students in the top two tiers.

Positive Behavior Intervention Strategies (PBIS): In recent years, emphasis has been placed on schools using evidence-based approaches to inappropriate school behavior. By enacting Positive Behavior Support (PBS) in a school, teachers and a Leadership Team can provide tailored intervention plans for specific groups of students. These intervention strategies use Functional Behavior Assessments to determine the cause and then identify ways to reduce or eliminate these behaviors.

Post-Traumatic Stress Disorder (PTSD): An anxiety disorder resulting from witnessing or experiencing an extremely traumatic life event such as physical or sexual abuse, a serious accident, a natural disaster, or military combat. Symptoms may include, but are not limited to, depression, recurring memories, aggressiveness, irritability, avoidance, irrational fears, and feelings of hopelessness.

Pre-Kindergarten (Pre-K): This refers to a non-compulsory program for children ages three to five to prepare them for kindergarten. Studies show that children who attend a well-planned Pre-K program are less likely to be held back or drop out of school and more likely to graduate. These programs are held in religious centers, public schools, private nursery schools, and child care centers. Teachers of Pre-K follow a structured program and teach not only academics but also emotional, social, and physical skills.

Preliminary Scholastic Assessment Test/ National Merit Scholarship Qualifying Test (PSAT/NMSQT): Co-sponsored by the College Board and National Merit Scholarship Corporation, this optional test serves as practice for the SAT and gives high school students the opportunity to compete for scholarships as well as to receive feedback on areas of strength or weakness.

Professional Learning Communities (PLC): A movement which is currently being used to create teams within schools that include the community to support the learning needs of the students. It is based on three big ideas developed by Richard DuFour. The ideas are: Ensuring that Students Learn; A Culture of Collaboration; and A Focus on Results. PLCs are typically focused on a particular strategy for teaching.

Project-Based Learning (PBL): This type of learning begins with a real world question and entices students to engage in their own exploration of the problem. There are seven elements that project-based learning should have: 1-a need to know; 2-a driving question; 3-student voice and choice; 4-21st century skills; 5-inquiry and innovation; 6-feedback and revision, and 7-a publicly presented product. This type of learning involves teachers as coaches or facilitators and students cooperatively working in pairs or groups and controlling the learning processes. This is not to be confused with problem-based learning (which does not include a project at the end).

Race to the Top (R2T): Education funding program initiated by the Obama administration and funded in part by stimulus money, it is designed to develop a set of national standards and to promote teacher evaluation based upon performance and student achievement. It also encourages the development of a larger number of charter schools.

Response to Intervention (RTI): This is a multi-level prevention system that is data driven and incorporates individual interventions for students who have needs or deficits in areas of learning or behavior. RTI first begins academically with administering a universal screening or pretest. This data is used to determine where students are in relation to a particular area of learning. Students are then grouped by tiers based on their competence. Three tiers are usually used as groupings. Those who need some sort of intervention are placed in Tier II while those who need the most intervention are placed in Tier III. Interventions are then put into place and monitored. Tiering is always fluid, and students can move throughout each tier as progress is made.

Scholastic Aptitude Test (SAT): Administered by the College Board, this standardized college entrance exam measures readiness in the areas of critical reading, math, and writing, as well as optional subject-specific tests. It is required by most colleges as part of the admissions process.

School Improvement Plan (SIP): This term can denote a state or federal mandated creation of an instructional plan or a plan that individual schools use to review, revise, and implement needed changes or improvements to their school. They can be completed yearly or in a two or three year cycle. The Virginia Department of Education defines it as "strategies and steps that a school will utilize to raise student achievement. A plan may involve new programs, more assistance for students, new curricula and/or teacher training."

SMART Goal: This mnemonic was created to help educators structure individual goals when developing projects. SMART stands for Specific, Measurable, Attainable, Realistic, and Time-Bound.

- *Specific*: Teachers need to be able to answer who, what, when, where, and why as the formulative goals. By being specific and precise, it increases the likelihood that teachers will be able to accomplish their goals.
- *Measurable*: It is important that teachers accurately assess progress in order to accomplish their ultimate objectives.
- *Attainable*: All goals should be achievable within a reasonable amount of time rather than in the distant future.
- *Relevant*: Teachers need to ensure that their goals are consistent with the current conditions of the school and with the realities of their student populations.
- *Time-Bound*: There always needs to be a deadline to ensure progress and completion of any goal.

Recently, "Evaluate" and "Reevaluate" have been added to the mnemonic which now reads SMARTER.

Special Education (SPED): Special education refers to specialized instruction tailored to a student's unique learning style. Special education services are provided for students with specific learning challenges ranging from developmental delays, specific learning disabilities, and sensory impairments so that the student may have access to the general education curriculum.

State Standards: The educational system in the United States is largely decentralized; states and private parties are responsible for the establishment of educational institutions and for defining curricula requirements. Thus, publically funded schools are held to standards that are established by their individual states. State standards are readily available online at the individual state Department of Education sites.

Student Council Association (SCA): Most elementary and secondary schools in the United States have established Student Council Associations. These governing associations are based on representative-based governments and are designed to help convey student interests and concerns to school administrators. Elections to the SCA are generally made by the student body and most organizations consist of a teacher sponsor, president, vice president, secretary, treasurer, and historian. The National Association of Student Councils (NASC) is the national coordinating organization in the United States while most states have separate associations to support local individual chapters.

Student Resource Officers (SRO): SROs are law enforcement officials that are placed within a school setting. They act as a law enforcement officer, law enforcement liaison, and/or a law enforcement educator. These individuals work closely with administrators, faculty, and staff to maintain safety within the school building and throughout the school property. SROs can also act as "points of contact" for the local law enforcement agency that they are connected with to ensure the safety of all students, faculty, and staff. SRO responsibilities are set by local law enforcement agencies.

Title I: Title I is a program established through the Elementary and Secondary Education Act that provides federal funding to schools with high percentages of students from low-income families. An entire school may be identified as Title I through a "schoolwide program", or schools may identify individual students through a "targeted assistance program." Additional funding and resources are provided for Title I identified students and schools. Visit www.ed.gov for more information.

Title II: Also a provision of the Elementary and Secondary Education Act, the purpose of Title II is to prepare, train, and recruit high quality teachers and principals. The federal government provides grants to state educational agencies and local educational agencies and organizations for higher education in order to improve the quality of school staff and hold schools accountable for student achievement. Visit www.ed.gov for more information.

Title III: Title III is officially known as the English Language Acquisition; Language Enhancement; and Academic Achievement Act and is part of the No Child Left Behind Law. The purpose of Title III is to use federal funding to help Limited English Proficiency (LEP) students improve their language proficiency and meet academic standards. Visit www. ed.gov for more information.

Title IX: This landmark provision was passed as part of the Educational Amendments of 1972 to address gender equality. Title IX asserts that "No person in the United States shall on the basis of sex, be excluded from participation in, be denied the benefits of, or be subjected to discrimination under any education program or activity receiving federal financial assistance." Title IX prevents discrimination in sports, admissions, counseling, etc. Visit www.

ed.gov for more information.

Tort Insurance: A tort is generally defined as a civil wrong doing which has resulted in

Title IX was passed in 1972 and has led to greater participation of girls in inter-scholastic sports and other extracurricular school activities. (Comstock Images)

a preceived harm or injury and which can result in litigation. Teachers can be sued for a variety of reasons including misconduct, failure to complete contracted duties, improper discipline, carelessness, negligence, improper supervision, causing physical or emotional injury, malpractice, and a myriad of other things. Legal insurance is offered by various teacher associations as part of membership dues.

United States Department of Education (ED, DoED): This federal agency's official abbreviation is "ED" (not "DOE," which refers to Department of Energy). The Department of Education's mission is "to promote student

The United States Department of Education was created in 1979 during the administration of President Jimmy Carter. (Philip Bigler)

achievement and preparation for global competitiveness by fostering educational excellence and ensuring equal access." The principle purposes of the department are to coordinate federal funding for education, collect data on U.S. schools, focus national attention on education issues, and enforce federal educational laws concerning privacy and civil rights. The official website of the United States Depart-

ment of Education is www.ed.gov.

Wechsler Intelligence Scale for Children (WISC): Designed by David Wechsler, this intelligence test measures the cognitive ability of children ages 6-16 and generates an IQ score based on verbal and nonverbal measures. It is used for identification screenings for gifted children and for diagnosis of learning disabilities.

Key Links

The Americans with Disabilities Act
http://www.ada.gov

The Association of American Educators
http://aaeteachers.org

The College Board
http://www.collegeboard.org

Learning Disabilities Association
http://ldanatl.org

National Autism Association
http://nationalautismassociation.org

National Center for Learning Disabilities
http://www.ncld.org

National Education Association
http://www.nea.org

Virginia Department of Education
http://www.doe.virginia.gov

United States Department of Education
http://www.ed.gov

Contributors

Linda Bigler
High School Spanish and Curriculum Resource Teacher, Fairfax County Public Schools
BA from The College of William & Mary/MA from George Mason University
email: lindabig@aol.com

Philip Bigler
High School History and Humanities, Fairfax County Public Schools
1998 National Teacher of the Year
1999 Milken National Educator Award
BA and M.Ed from James Madison University/MA from The College of William & Mary
email: philipbigler@yahoo.com

Susan Catlett
Chemistry Teacher, Spotsylvania County Public Schools
2010 Region III Teacher of the Year
BA and M.Ed from The College of William & Mary
email: susan0824@gmail.com

Susanne Dana
Chemistry Teacher, Montgomery County Schools
2012 American Chemical Society Southeast Regional Award for Excellence in High School Teaching
2008 Region VI Teacher of the Year
National Board Certified
BS and MS from Virginia Tech
email: sdana@mcps.org

Jami Dodenhoff
Second Grade Teacher, Prince William County Schools
2009 Teacher of Promise
BS and MAT from James Madison University
2010 Teacher of Promise
email: jamildodenhoff@gmail.com

Stephanie Doyle
History Teacher, Roanoke City Schools
2009 Virginia Teacher of the Year
BA from Roanoke College/MA from Walden University
email: vatoy09@yahoo.com

Karen Drosinos
Kindergarten Teacher, Virginia Beach Public Schools
2011 Region II Teacher of the Year
2013 Virginia Lottery Super Teacher Award
National Board Certified
BS from Penn State University/MA University of Maryland
email: Karen.Drosinos@VBSchools.com

Kathy Galford
Sixth Grade English, Chesapeake Public Schools
2013 Virginia Teacher of the Year
BS and MEd from Old Dominion University
email: kathy.galford@cpschools.com

Carolyn Lewis
Primary Teacher Second Grade, Amelia County Public Schools
2010 Region VIII Teacher of the Year
BS from Longwood University/MEd from Regent University
email: cdlewis49@gmail.com

Raegan Rangel
Principal, Frederick County Public Schools
2003 Milken National Educator Award
BA from Shenandoah University and MA from George Mason University
email: rangelr@frederick.k12.va.us

Katie Overstreet Ruscito
School Counselor, Clarke County Schools
2006 Teacher of Promise
BS from James Madison University/M.Ed and Ed. S in school counseling from James Madison University
email: ruscitok@clarke.k12.va.us

Suzi Sherman
Second Grade Teacher, King William County Schools
2013 Region III Teacher of the Year
BS from Virginia Commonwealth University/MS from the Medical College of VA./Certificate in Teaching from the University of Richmond
email: ssherman@kwcps.k12.va.us

Tabitha Strickler
English Teacher, Colonial Heights City
2008 Region I Teacher of the Year
BA from The College of William & Mary/MEd from the University of Virginia
email: tabitha.strickler@gmail.com

Cathy Webb
Speech Language Pathologist/Austism Instructor,
 Giles County Public Schools
2010 Virginia Teacher of the Year
BA and MA from Marshall University/Certificate Autism Studies from Regent University
email: cwebb@gilesk12.org

(Not pictured: Raegan Rangel, Katie Overstreet Ruscito, Cathy Webb)

VAT🍎Y

Stephanie Doyle, Philip Bigler, and Karen Drosinos are the primary editors of *Teaching is Tough!* They serve as part of the leadership team for the Virginia Teacher of the Year Network (VATOY) and have collaborated on a variety of educational projects and initiatives, including the Virginia Teaching, Leadership, and Collaboration Symposium and the annual statewide Teacher of the Year recognition reception. Stephanie, the 2009 Virginia Teacher of the Year, is currently a middle school social studies teacher at Breckinridge Middle School in Roanoke City and is the chairperson of the Virginia Teacher of the Year Network. Philip Bigler was chosen as the 1998 National Teacher of the Year during a Rose Garden Ceremony hosted by President Bill Clinton. Recently retired after 35 years in public education, Bigler taught high school history/ humanities in Fairfax County and later served as the director of the James Madison Center for Liberty & Learning at James Madison University. He is the author of nine books including his memoir, *Teaching History in an Uncivilized World*. Karen has been recognized as the 2011 Region II Teacher of the Year and has also received the Virginia State Lottery Super Teacher award as well as the Penn State Outstanding Teacher Award. She teaches kindergarten at Pembroke Elementary School in Virginia Beach and serves as the Vice Chair for VATOY.

INDEX

(Media Focus)

The Margaret Sue Copenhaver Institute

Supporting educators as they seek to foster within students a lifelong love of learning.

> "Education is not the filling of a pail, but the lighting of a fire."
>
> -William Butler Yeats

The Margaret Sue Copenhaver Institute for Teaching and Learning is an **annual teacher professional development program** offered at Roanoke College in Salem, Virginia. Each June, the Institute offers a learner-centered approach to professional development.

Moving away from a workshop approach, the Institute's three-day professional development opportunity helps classroom practitioners construct new knowledge and understanding about teaching and learning through trusting, interdependent interaction with peers and experts at all levels of schooling. The approach is based on the principles that teachers learn best when a shared vision guides the decisions and programs of teacher development, when college faculty act as facilitators of knowledge, and when participants are actively engaged in the professional development process.

MSCI is a proud partner of the Virginia Teacher of the Year Network.

**Find out more at
www.roanoke.edu/msci**

COPENHAVER
INSTITUTE
ROANOKE COLLEGE

134